Not Just George

by John Lyons

Foreword by Sir David Jason OBE

ISBN: 978-1-7358118-8-8

Publisher Acknowledgments

First, and foremost we want to thank the author, John Lyons for sharing his story with us. He's a class act (pun fully intended) and we're happy to be a part of his journey.

We would also like to thank Micky Mamuzelos for his work on the cover. Stunning as always.

And we couldn't do any of the things we do without our partners and friends, Rick and Beverley Mayston at Agent Fox Media Limited. Thanks to both of you for all of your hard work on this project.

Finally, Jerry Mooney and I (The Mooney and Lambert in Mooney and Lambert) would like to thank our spouses and the other members of our team who provide second sets of eyes, extra work, and patience as we take time from our lives to tell the stories of others.

We hope you, dear reader, enjoy this book as much as we have. Check out our other titles, and what is coming next, at mooneyandlambert.com.

Now Let's go. Chop, chop! Enjoy the story of the life of John Lyons, a prolific and delightful actor who has, and continues to, delight thousands upon thousands with his performances from film to television, to the stage.

Troy Lambert and Jerry Mooney

Foreword from Sir David Jason OBE

Having known John Lyons (or West End Johnny as I like to call him), for a number of years, I know this book will be an uplifting and cheerful read just as he is a cheerful and uplifting person. He has led a long and varied career and has many a tale to tell. I first met him when we worked together on A Touch of Frost – he played Sergeant George Toolan to my Detective Inspector Frost. We had so many laughs along the way and he was a great team member, always with a story or two to entertain us all. I am pleased therefore that he has put so many of his anecdotes down in print and is ready to share his journey over the years by way of this book. Sit back, relax and enjoy the read.

Contents

Foreword from Sir David Jason OBE . . . 4

Acknowledgments 6

Chapter One: A Very Noisy Beginning . . 7

Chapter Two: Jack the Ripper. 9

Chapter Three:
Growing Up in The East End. 11

Chapter Four: School. 19

Chapter Five:
Very Nearly a Silly Mistake 22

Chapter Six: Ronnie and Reggie 25

Chapter Seven: A Wonderful Happening. . 29

Chapter Eight: A Chance Encounter . . . 32

Chapter Nine:
Drama School - The Audition 35

Chapter Ten:
Three Years of Drama School 37

Chapter Eleven: Going Out
Into The Big World of Showbiz 40

Chapter Twelve:
A Long and Varied Career 48

Chapter Thirteen: Ridley and Me 63

Chapter Fourteen: Not All Work 74

Chapter Fifteen: The High Seas. 77

Chapter Sixteen: Lionel Bart And Joan . 91

Chapter Seventeen: Jobs I Didn't Get. . 99

Chapter Eighteen:
A Second String to My Bow 110

Chapter Nineteen: Luck or Fate? 117

Chapter Twenty:
Come Along George, Chop-Chop 124

Chapter Twenty-One:
Back on The Boards 143

Chapter Twenty-Two:
Cruising with P & O 158

Chapter Twenty-Three: Out on Tour . . . 161

Acknowledgments

With many thanks to Ann, my wife, and Laura, my daughter, for their help in getting this book together.

Plus my agent, Patsy Martin and her husband Maurice at Personal Appearances for both their help and encouragement.

Chapter One:
A Very Noisy Beginning

Every story has to start somewhere, mine started at 2am on the morning of Monday September 14th, 1943, Mary Rosetta Lyons was about to give birth to her third child.

At the same time Field Marshal Goering had ordered his Luftwaffe Division out on one of its many sorties to bomb the docks and surrounding area of London's East End, the object being to cut off one of the major routes of supplies into London and therefore the country, and to demoralise its citizens.

Well, it did not demoralise Mary Rosetta Lyons, who chose not to join my father, brother and sister, in taking safety in the shelter of the basement of the only factory left standing in the area. Instead, she chose to remain in her bedroom along with a midwife, and my Aunt Nell. At the time, bombs were dropping all around 48 Wodeham Street, Whitechapel - which was one of only three houses left standing, when I made my entrance into the world.

Many years before, Wodeham Street had been called Queen Anne Street. All my mother's family lived down that street. My mother being the youngest of 17 children. Can you imagine that?

Two of the questions I often get asked are, how did I become an actor, and were any of your family in show business before you? Well, the answer to that second question is most certainly no. My father Jack worked as a crane driver at St Katherine's Dock alongside Tower Bridge. In fact, all my family on both my father and mother's side all worked in one capacity or another in the London Docks.

My father got my elder brother Joe employed there when he left school at fifteen, and that was going to be my fate when I reached that age. He did in fact get me an interview with the PLA – Port of London Authority - which turned out to be a written exam. Which believe me was not very difficult. But for some reason, I deliberately failed it. I am not quite sure why, because I had no plans for the future, very little education, and certainly no qualifications (I hadn't even passed my 11 Plus). Most certainly I never thought about becoming an actor. This decision to deliberately fail that exam, proved to be a great disappointment to my father.

Chapter Two:
Jack the Ripper

My mother on the other hand was a cleaning lady, working at nights scrubbing the basement floors of the Royal London Hospital in Whitechapel for many years. So, that is where I was born – in that little house in the middle of a bomb site behind Whitechapel Station, with an outside toilet, no heating, and no bath - you had to throw everything in the sink.

As the years went on, that area became the stomping ground of Ronnie and Reggie – the Kray twins. In fact, they lived in the next road to me – 178 Vallance Road (Fort Vallance). Many years later I was to have a lifesaving encounter with the twins which I shall recall later. Back in the year 1888 that area became infamous as the stalking ground of Jack the Ripper.

At that time, although my mother had not been born yet, all her family lived in Queen Anne Street. On one dark November morning at 4am, my grandfather – another Jack – who at that time drove a horse and cart delivering coal (how he found the time I will never know, having fathered seventeen kids) he left home, walked up Queen Anne Street, and turned left into what then was Bucks Row (now Durward Street).

On stopping at the yard where the horses were kept, to his surprise, he could not get the gates open, owing to a large

Not Just George

mound of rags, paper and tarpaulin. So, he started pushing away all the rubbish with his foot and to his great surprise, and horror, there emerged the body of a woman who had been cut from head to toe, with her body parts lying alongside her.

Of course, he jumped six feet in the air, and ran to the nearest street, where he knew he would find a Bobby on the beat – Brady Street. He brought him back, showed him what he had found, and quickly left.

That body turned out to be the mutilated body of Mary Ann Nicholls – known as Polly. As you can see, I had quite a few aunts, uncles, and cousins. All of whom told me that story – probably a bit embellished along the way. So, legend has it, my grandfather, was the very first person to find the very first victim of Jack the Ripper. And that's the closest anyone in my family ever got to show business.

Chapter Three:
Growing Up in The East End

So, that's where I was born, and that's where I lived with my parents, my brother and sister. In those years of growing up, I became a great burden, and caused quite a lot of trouble for my parents. I first became a problem at the early age of five, when my sister Kit, who was fourteen years older, took me to my first day of school, in nearby Hanbury Street. After she had deposited me in the classroom, I created such a scene that the lovely old grey-haired teacher, grabbed me by the arms, in the hope of calming me down.

I then (and I do regret it) kicked her very hard in the shins and ran. When my sister arrived home, I was sitting on the kitchen floor, eating a slice of bread and jam. That poor elderly teacher never returned to school again.

I wasn't a very happy boy at school, I would play truant most days, which meant the school board officer would turn up at our door enquiring "Where's your young boy Johnny?" I can tell you where Johnny was, in the West End. Soho to be precise. I had found a way of prising open the back of my mother's glass cabinet in which she kept a jar of three-penny and six-penny pieces under lock and key, and I stole them. She never did find out. I would spend days roaming the streets of Soho with other boys.

Not Just George

Can you imagine what trouble that could have led to for young boys of twelve and thirteen? I shudder to think. One particular boy (Barry) and I got on very well together. We would often disappear to Southend, spend the night sleeping rough on the beach, then hitching a ride back to London the next day. Or we would make our way to Kent, steal some fruit from a farm, spend the night in a bus shelter, before making our way back home. All without telling our parents.

Barry and I got into what could have become a profoundly serious problem. We had got the train from Bethnal Green to Chingford, and just walked through Epping Forest with no particular goal in mind. At the time we both had air guns in our pockets which looked very much like the real thing, but only fired lead slugs, which could hurt, especially if hit in the face. Suddenly we came across five teenagers about the same age as us (three boys and two girls). For no reason, and we certainly hadn't planned it, we held them up like two highwaymen.

When I come to think of it now, Epping Forest was the hiding place of the most famous Highwayman of all, Dick Turpin. That's where he started his famous ride to York on his horse Black Bess. Anyway, whilst getting them to sit down in a circle, one of boys got up and made a run for it, quickly disappearing through the woods. Half an hour later, when the other four had emptied their pockets on the ground, five great big hairy policemen came running over the hill, followed by the one boy who had escaped. Off we both fled leaving everything behind, but not the police, they were close on our tails. Barry went one way, I the other.

Barry was very quickly caught, but I outran the slightly overweight policeman chasing me, and made it to Chingford Station. There was the train waiting to leave. I jumped in, slammed the door, and prayed it would pull away quickly before Mr Policeman caught up with me. It did, and I was back in Whitechapel within the hour. By the time I reached the top of our street, there was a police car outside our front door, with two police officers talking to my poor dear mum. Barry had told them where I lived. I don't blame him. We weren't exactly the Mafia with a code of silence.

We were then both taken to the local Police Station, the air guns confiscated, and given a very stern talking to, and a stark warning about our futures. We were both incredibly lucky that time, but not the next. We hadn't learnt our lesson. On a sunny afternoon after playing cricket in the street, someone came up with the bright idea of breaking into the local hospital. This was a hospital that stood on the corner of Vallance Road and Fulbourne Street and had been bombed ten or twelve years earlier during the Second World War. All that was left now, was an exceptionally large bomb site, on which all the local kids played.

The whole site was surrounded by a large wall, but in one corner stood a large four-storey building that was still being used, but no one knew what for. Six of us squeezed through a small window of the cellar at the back and wandered slowly upstairs looking for anything of interest. We were not professional burglars and had very little idea what we were looking for, or what we would do with it if we found it. On reaching the top floor, we forced open the door of a very large room. There, in cages on all sides of the room were animals of all types: mice, guinea pigs, rats, and at the far end, big white rabbits.

No one wanted anything to do with the mice, rats, or guinea pigs – but the rabbits looked nice and cuddly. Three of the boys opened the cages and wanted to take some of them home, which they did. I am glad to say, I didn't touch them at all.

Not Just George

We learnt later, after we had all been caught, that that building was used as a laboratory for the London Hospital to carry out tests and experiments for various diseases and new drugs. Now this had become serious. Those boys who had come into contact with the animals were admitted into hospital for tests, whilst the other three of us were given a two-week sentence in Stamford House Reform Centre Shepherds Bush. That two weeks taught me a lesson I did not want to repeat. What with early morning cold showers, cold food, history lessons, and a fight every night in the large, cold dormitory where we all slept. No thank you.

At home, things seem to carry on as before. I was one of those little urchins who stood outside on the pavement of pubs asking for a bag of crisps and lemonade to keep me quiet. Mum and dad were having a knees up inside with all the regulars. Not that my mum and dad went out very often, money would have been very tight. Plus, I always had the feeling that by now they were not getting along very well. They didn't seem to talk to each other very much. My dad would always go to the pub before coming home from work, and it was always my job to go to Murphy's at Mile End Gate, poke my head around the corner and say "Dad! Mum says are you coming home for dinner?"

By the time we got home, he would be noticeably quiet and slightly drunk. Dinner would be cold. This obviously was very frustrating for my mother, after working throughout the night scrubbing floors and then coming home, sorting out the housework in the morning, trying to get a few hours' sleep in the afternoon, and then up again around 5pm to look after me, my elder brother Joe and dad.

On one occasion she lost it completely and went for my father, who was sitting at the kitchen table, with a beer bottle

in hand. I, without thinking, jumped in between them, and prevented what could have been a very nasty incident.

14

John Lyons

When I say my mum and dad never seemed to talk much to one another, it also seemed to filter down to myself and my brother (my sister Kit, who was fourteen years older than me, had left and was married by now). They just didn't seem to have the skills or words to be able to communicate or show their feelings. I'm sure this was the same for most working-class families in the 1940s and 50s. I myself received very little advice on anything, but I'm sure in their own way, there was love and feeling they just didn't know how to show.

I cannot remember my mum ever putting her arms around me (although she did throw me down the stairs once out of pure frustration). A typical frustration may well have occurred one Christmas morning, when, my presents on that day were my first pair of long trousers, and a great pair of roller skates. Both presents must have, at that time, cost my parents quite a bit of hard-earned cash.

Of course, I couldn't wait to get those trousers on, strap up my new skates, get out on the street, and show off to all the boys. By lunch time, I'm back home, trousers ripped on both knees, one of the wheels missing from the left skate, and blood running from my right hand, where I had tried to stop myself falling. I don't blame my mum being angry, but throwing me down the stairs, was perhaps a little excessive, don't you think?

I can only ever remember my dad saying "You're a good boy Johnny," when two nights before he died, I took him a hot drink and a hot water bottle into his bed. (I was by now aged twenty and I hope a different person). When he did pass away two days later in hospital, a very young policeman came round to tell my mum that her husband had died and placed all his belongings on the kitchen table. One shilling and four old pennies.

Not Just George

I can still see myself staring at them. Not much for forty-five years of work would you say? For a man who had never missed a day's work in his life, or stole anything at all from the Port of London Authority?

One incident I do remember with my father, happened when I was about the age of twelve. We were in our small kitchen at home, and I must have upset him in some way, because I remember him coming towards me with his hands raised. I was now fairly tall and beginning to develop some muscle, I squared up to him ready to have fight. I remember the complete look of shock on his face, that his twelve-year-old son, would think of wanting to fight him. That must have hurt him greatly. It certainly is something that I'm very ashamed of.

We did have one or two family holidays throughout the 40s and 50s, mainly the odd caravan holiday, or as a special treat, Butlin's. That was great. As a ten-year-old child, I had great fun at Butlin's, even sleeping in a top bunk bed, with my brother below was an adventure. I would spend the days on all the rides, swimming, playing football, and joining in all the other activities going. The highlight being the evening when we all got dressed up and went for dinner at our allotted time.

After that, it would be for me, straight to the show theatre to watch whatever entertainment was on offer that night. I remember seeing some great shows there. An early Charlie Drake, when he worked as a double act (Mick & Montmorency) a very young Jimmy Tarbuck. But for me, Morecambe & Wise for some reason stood out. I was only ten, couldn't understand half of their many jokes, but somehow, I knew they were very good, and very funny. It must have been their spot-on timing, and the way they bounced jokes off each other. Wonderful.

John Lyons

Most of all, my big treat of the year was hop picking. At that time, most East End families left London for the hop fields of Kent, during the long school holidays through August to the end of September. Mums and kids would stay the whole time, sleeping in small huts, and sleeping on a straw mattress, with all the cooking done on big open fires outside. My job each day was to go and fetch the wood faggots for the fire. The husbands would be back up in London working at their various jobs and travel down by train from Victoria Station to Paddock Wood on Friday nights, returning back to London on Sunday nights.

So, Friday and Saturday nights were times to relax and enjoy themselves. The local Pub, The Rose & Crown next door to what was, and still is, the Hoppers Hospital, was full and loud with singing and drinking. This was of course, just a few years after the Second World War. So, everyone felt entitled to a bit of fun and relief.

One particular year most of my very large family travelled down together with my Uncle Art (short for Arthur) bringing down with him an old piano on the back of his lorry. We spent many evenings sitting round that piano by the fire singing everything and anything. My sister Kit was top of the bill.

She not only had a good singing voice but could play the piano (a bit) she was a young Vera Lynn. When the end of the hop picking season came around, instead of loading up and taking the piano home with him, Uncle Art just chucked it on the fire. We all watched it burn (what a fine way to treat a Steinway!). He was the uncle who took great pleasure in teaching me to swear. And I took great pleasure in repeating it. Now, I only swear when I stub my toe in the middle of the night. But then we all do that.

How's this for a boy of nine? The doorbell goes one afternoon at 48 Wodeham street, and I'm playing on the floor of the back bedroom. It's my mum's two elder sisters, Betty and Ellen, dressed up to the nines. Before anyone else can answer it, I lift up the back window, poke my head out and shout, "What do you two fucking Russian whores want?" What a well-mannered lad I must have been. Fifty-five years later, I find myself having a cosy chat, with our dear Queen, and Prince Phillip in the West End. Ho ho.

When I say hop picking, I didn't do much picking, but I found great freedom running around the fields, playing on old tractors, and feeding and chasing sheep. One of the highlights of the day was the passing through of the Golden Arrow train. This was the continental train which left Victoria Station bound for Dover and then by ferry on to France. The cry would go up, and everyone would rush to the fence to see this wonderful big train, with its large golden arrow emblem on the front, speed on by. Always giving a long blast on its hooter. What a wonderful sight!

Chapter Four:
School

It was always a very sad time when the hop picking season came to an end and we all returned to London. For me, at the age of eleven, this meant a new school, Cephas Secondary Modern, Bethnal Green.

This was a very hard place. Full of boys and girls, who, like me, had not passed our 11 Plus exam. I learnt very little over the next four years, what with boys throwing desks at teachers, and finding myself in a long line of boys outside the Headmaster's office, waiting for your turn to receive the cane.

Back in the fifties, teachers were allowed to give the cane whenever they saw fit, and most of them saw fit quite often. One teacher in particular had his own method. He was the P.E. teacher. His name I have long forgotten. You would have to cross your hands, palms up, and with his running shoe turned round, he would bring it down as hard as he could, using the heel of the slipper. Oh, it did hurt. But not as much as when you were sent to the Headmaster's office. His idea of punishment was to have you hold out your left hand, and with a thin cane, bring it down hard on the tips of your fingers. His extra bit of fun was, before he brought it down, he would jump in the air, to give it maximum weight on the downward stroke. That really did sting.

As soon as us boys could get out of his office, we would be down those stairs, into the playground, straight into the boys' toilets, and pee on your hands, in the hope of taking the sting away. So, if you should meet me at anytime, anywhere, it might be wise not to shake hands.

The teachers tried their best, but there was very little discipline or motivation. I was very good, if I do say so myself, at kiss chase and football. In that order. But there wasn't much of a career in that. At one point my dad suggested I should join the Boy Scouts. So, mum enrolled me into the local Scout group at Toynbee Hall, after having invested in the full Scout uniform. I'm sorry to say, that by the end of the first week, I had punched another boy in the mouth, and I was thrown out. Richard was his name. Richard, if ever you read this, and remember me, I apologise.

I myself am not a violent man, but like a lot of people, I do have a temper, which I normally keep well under control. The one thing that makes me see red, is bullying. Whilst at school I had a boy sitting next to me by the name of Roberts. A rather slight boy, who was being bullied all the time, particularly by one boy in the class, who would not leave him alone.

Now, Roberts' nickname was Soapy, which I must say was about right. He did smell. Other boys in the class refused to sit next to him, but I felt sorry for him, and put up with it. I was never bullied, one of the reasons I think, is that I was on the school boxing team, had three fights, all three of which I had won, and became East London boxing champion for my weight (in that third fight, I received such a punch on the nose which brought tears to my eyes, and that was the end of my boxing career).

I noticed one day, Roberts giving this other boy his money. A strange thing to do, as he could have had very little himself. It happened the following week again. When I asked Roberts why he was giving his money away, He said if he didn't, the other boy (who I won't name) was going to beat

John Lyons

him up. This made me see red. A week later, I saw Roberts going into the boy's toilet in the school playground, followed by the unnamed bully. As I walked in, money was being handed over. That was it. I remember taking two steps towards them and hit the bully right in the mouth as hard as I could. I probably said a few choice words, picked up the money off the floor, and gave it back to Roberts, leaving the other boy holding his mouth. Roberts was never bullied again, and that other boy never said another word to me for the next year, when we all finally left. A typical coward.

Chapter Five:
Very Nearly a Silly Mistake

The only other time I got involved, could have turned out very nasty. It was mid-eighties, and I'm driving to my Solicitors office in Holborn. On reaching "Gray's Inn Road" I pulled up at the traffic lights behind another car. While waiting for the lights to change, I notice, on the opposite side of the road, two Mediterranean looking men, sitting at the lights in an open top Mini, with the music playing as loud as could be, (can you see the picture? Annoying isn`t it?)

As the Mini pulled away, it did a very sharp left turn, which is when I noticed that alongside it was a young boy on a scooter, who, trying to avoid the Mini turning, stumbled on the kerb, and fell. He, very stupidly, picked up an empty drink can from the gutter, and threw it at the car. Now, the can being empty, just travelled a few yards, and fell short.

That was enough for the two men in the Mini. They stopped, both got out, grabbed the boy, and threw him backwards into the plate glass window of a sweet shop. As the kid hit the wall, the helmet he was wearing fell off, and long hair fell to his shoulders. From the point of view I had from across the road, to me it looked like a girl, not a boy. That for me was when the red mist descended. I reversed back, swerved around the car in front, and went across the road without looking. I jumped out, and, like "Starsky & Hutch" flew across the bonnet of my car (at this point, I had forgotten who I was, or where).

John Lyons

It's amazing how in moments like this, adrenalin pumps through your body, and you seem to have the strength of two men. I came off my bonnet, landed on my feet, and with my whole weight and forward momentum behind me, caught the first man coming towards me with a right hand punch, flush on his nose. He went flying backwards towards the wall, and I turned to engage the second man, who was now almost on top of me. He, I caught with a left hook, that Mike Tyson would have been proud of. He went off the floor in a sitting position for about two seconds and finished on his backside on the pavement.

As he hit the pavement, both blood and teeth flew out of his mouth. I now turn to face the first man, but he is not there. He's had enough. He is now fifty yards up the road, leaning against a post, with blood pouring out of his nose. He was out of the game. Lucky for me, because, as I turn to face the second one, he is coming at me again. This time, he got a right hook straight in the left eye, which again sent him back to the wall. As I moved towards him, he very quickly put one arm up in the air and said "Enough, enough, I'm sorry, I'm sorry."

I grabbed him by the collar and said, "Don't apologise to me, say sorry to that young kid". He did, and I sent him on his way to pick up his friend, who was fifty yards up the road, to get in their car, and piss off quick. Or words to that effect, which they did. I then picked up the boy's helmet, gave it back to him, and send him on his way. A strange thing that has stayed in my mind.

When I looked around, it seemed as though the whole road had stopped as one. Heads were sticking out of the betting shop door, buses had pulled up to watch, mums with prams, but nobody said a word. They just stared, wondering where this crazy fella had come from. I then went around to my driver's door, opened it and got in. That's when I came back to my senses. For there, in the passenger seat, sat my seven-year-old daughter. She watched her dad, fighting with two strange men, on the pavement in the middle of London. I remember saying to her "I'm sorry darling, I hope you weren't frightened?"

"No dad, it just frightened me when you drove across the road without looking."

My word. On thinking about it that night, and ever since, I have often thought what could have happened, if that first man had got his punch in first, or, even worse, if one of them had a weapon of some sort. With my daughter having a grandstand view, it doesn't bear thinking about.

I hope you believe what you have just read? I know it reads like something out of a film, but it is all true, word for word. Laura my daughter, is my witness. I have over the years tried my best to mind my own business, but it's not always easy. I'm sure we all have to bite our tongues, when on a bus, or a train, and we hear a man or woman swearing while on their mobile phone. Or even in the queue at the supermarket, and the person in front is being rude to the girl behind the till. I know I do. I often have to remind myself, "John, you're not twenty-five anymore, you're an OAP!"

Chapter Six:
Ronnie and Reggie

Before I leave my teenage years, I would like to recall my encounter with 'The Twins' – Ronnie and Reggie. As I said before, the twins lived in the next street to me. Me, in Wodeham Street, they in Vallance Road. So, you would see them about with "The Firm", which was what the gang were called, quite a bit. Of course, everybody knew who they were. Our age difference was about fourteen years at this time, them, at the age of twenty- seven, and me at this time in 1956, a young thirteen.

One cold rainy night, myself and three other boys are bunking into the back of the Essoldo Cinema in the Bethnal Green Road. We were hoping to see Brigitte Bardot in the film "God Created Women." At this time, at the young age of thirteen, I am a big fan, as most teenagers were, of the actor James Dean. I'm dressed in a leather jacket, jeans, white T-shirt and a crew neck jumper.

On leaving the cinema that night, we began walking home down Vallance Road. Now you can imagine, four young boys laughing and giggling over what we had just seen on the screen, when suddenly from behind appeared a gang of older boys – or men really. We are thirteen, they are probably twenty-one. A big difference at that age.

The leader, for some reason, stepped up to me and said, "You looking for trouble John?" Now, John is just an expression, it's not that he knew my name.

I remember replying "No, no… we've just come out of the pictures."

With that, from behind his back came half a house brick and the words "fucking liar." He then hit me right on the top of the head. My legs buckled, but I didn't go all the way down. I sprang up just in time to see my three friends scatter, and half of the other gang go after them. Instinct told me to run as well. I did. As fate would have it, I ran to my left down Vallance Road, with the rest of that gang close behind me.

I probably had gone about sixty or seventy yards down the road, when the effect of that brick to the head, started to kick in, and, my running body slowly leaning forward, I fell face first into the gutter. As I fell, they caught up with me, and I saw one of them had an old glass milk bottle in his hand. This is where James Dean came to my rescue. I pulled the crew neck jumper over my head just in time, as the milk bottle smashed into my forehead and broke. I could feel the blood running down my face, and I tried to pull the leather jacket up as far as it would go. It was a good move.

The boy who had broken the bottle over my head, was now trying to get the jagged top of the bottle into my neck. At the same time, a knife was trying to get through to my back, with only little success thanks to the thickness of the leather jacket. It did draw blood, but thanks to that jacket – it could have been fatal. Meanwhile the rest are kicking and punching the rest of my body – arms and legs.

Now this beating only lasted about one and a half minutes, I guess. Strangely I couldn't feel any pain – they were hitting me so hard. Suddenly it stopped. Almost as quick as it started. I heard footsteps disappear into the night. I took a chance, slowly raised my head and I am now looking at the railway bridge halfway down Vallance Road. To me, it seemed covered in mist. As I turned my head to the left, still lying in the gutter – there stood a man in the doorway of his house with the passage light on behind him. I could see he was wearing, black slacks, a white shirt with both sleeves rolled up, open neck and braces. That image still stays with me.

By the grace of God, or fate – whatever – I had had the great fortune to run towards, and collapse on the doorstop of 178 Vallance Road – the home where Ronnie and Reggie lived with their mother Violet. Here was the reason that this gang had very quickly left me. They all knew who this man was – it was Reggie Kray. He very gently helped me out of the gutter, took me into 178, through to the small scullery in the back, while uttering words I couldn't even spell at the time.

He proceeded to patch me up and ask me "Where do you live son? I'll take you home."

I said "No, no – my mum would kill me."

"You need stitches to the back of your head and your back. I'd better take you to the hospital." He patched me up the best he could, we got into his car, and made the short ride to the Royal London Hospital in Whitechapel Road.

Having pulled up the ramp outside the main doors, he leant over, opened the passenger door and said, "You better go in yourself son, otherwise they might think I did it." He then, pushed me out.

So for me, that fateful night, the Gods were with me. I was wearing thick clothing, and after being hit on the head, I ran LEFT down Vallance Road, and not RIGHT. When I finally did collapse on the Kray's doorstep Reggie was in, heard the commotion, and came out, which I am sure saved my life. As a P.S to this story, four years later, the fella who hit me over the head with the milk bottle (whose name I

now knew) and then proceeded to try to get the rest of it
into my neck, was at a dance at York Hall Public Baths
when a soldier had said something to his girlfriend that he
took offence to. He followed that soldier into the men's
toilet, and promptly slit his throat with a knife, killing him
– he got life in prison. So, you can see, they weren't joking.
Some months later, I learnt, they thought I was someone
else. Sorry lads, my fault.

Chapter Seven:
A Wonderful Happening

Now dear reader, I tell you these troubling tales of my past, not because I'm proud of them (I most certainly am not) but to give you an inkling of what the future held in store for me. The Rocky Road that was ahead of me. (At least two of my friends at that time finished up spending time in prison). For me, on leaving school at the age of fifteen, something wonderful happened.

It's New Year's Eve 1958, I'm fifteen years old, and seeing the New Year in at the Blind Beggar Pub, Mile End Gate. At eleven o'clock that night, for some reason, I don't know why, I decided to go home, which was only ten minutes away. On getting home and sitting down for a few moments, something told me to go back. I'm so glad I did. For there I met, and got talking to, a young girl who I had seen around the area a few times, but never spoken to before. That night, after the New Year had been welcomed in, I walked her home, and she gave me the telephone number where she worked in the City of London. Advance 1221 (I still remember it now)

I called the next day, and we started going out together. For the next seven years we were, as they say, courting, and in 1965 we got married and we celebrated our Golden Wedding anniversary in 2015. So, meeting Ann that night, and a chance meeting with a journalist, led me into a completely different life. I'm seventeen, just coming up to eighteen, and working not in the London Docks, but for British Rail at Paddington Station.

A quick detour - while working for British Rail, I was assigned to the Long Iron Route. This was the delivery of long iron used in the construction of very tall buildings. This very heavy material was transported on the biggest lorry in the company, which required a very experienced driver, and his mate, me.

On this particular day, we are on our way to a construction site in the City of London, but, on this occasion, the regular driver was on annual leave, so was replaced by a less experienced one. On our way up Pentonville Road, passing the Angel, then descending down City Road, I noticed the new driver pumping furiously on the brake pedal. Somehow, the air pipes at the back of the cab that feed the brakes, were failing, and we are going downhill, picking up speed all the time, WITHOUT BRAKES.

Ahead of us at the traffic lights, were a couple of cars, and three big lorries waiting for the lights to change. There was no way now of warning anyone, or of missing them, we were going to hit them, full on, at speed. At the very last second, just before we hit the first lorry, the driver pulled the cab to his right, which meant, my side of the cab would take the full impact. It did. I instinctively, jumped from my seat, over the big engine that separated the two of us, and finished on top of my driver.

As I did this, the seat I had been sitting in a few seconds before, was ripped out, which would have taken my legs with it. Plus, the very heavy iron on the long loader behind us, came crashing through the back window of the cab, where I, again a few seconds before, had just been sitting. The strange thing about this incident is, although I was not physically hurt, for some reason I couldn't, and still can't remember anything that happened afterwards.

John Lyons

Was I taken to the hospital for a check-up? Was I interviewed about the crash? Did I give a statement to the police? Or did I go straight home, as if nothing had happened?

That whole mess would have taken quite a bit of cleaning up, roads closed, heavy lifting gear etc. One thing I do remember is, that no one in the vehicles in front of us, was seriously injured. This all happened well over sixty years ago, and I seemed to have put it completely out of my mind. Perhaps that's a good thing. Delayed shock? Maybe, who knows. Strange how the brain works.

Chapter Eight:
A Chance Encounter

On Sunday mornings along with thousands of other men and boys, I am playing football for a small pub side on the famous Hackney Marshes. As luck, or the famous fate would have it, an older chap joined this pub side by the name of Tom Duncan. Now at this time, Tom was the editor of the show page in our local paper "The East London Advertiser" which gave out news of all entertainment going on in the area.

One Thursday night after football training, I found myself sitting alongside Tom in the pub opposite. At this time, Tom had only been with us for a couple of months, which meant we didn't know each other too well. For some reason (and I never did ask why) he turned to me and said, "Tell me John, have you ever thought of becoming an actor?"

Well, this is the last thing I had ever thought of becoming. He then produced, from his wallet a card, and told me about a new drama school which would be opening in a couple of months' time at the Theatre Royal Stratford East, the home of Joan Littlewood's very well-respected company, Theatre Workshop. He suggested I should give them a call.

I wish I had asked him what he saw in me at the time, but I never did. A few months later he left our team, and I never saw him again. Two days later, I am sitting on the sidings of Paddington Station eating my sandwiches and holding the card that Tom had given me. I looked over the road and saw one of those old red telephone boxes with the old-fashioned A and B buttons. I thought about this for a few minutes, then plucked up the courage to call the number.

Luckily, I got through to the secretary of the theatre. A lovely lady by the name of Carol Murphy – who was at the time married to an actor in the company by the name of Brian Murphy. Many people will remember Brian many years later in the successful programme, George and Mildred. Carol explained to me all the plans and hopes that they had for this new drama school, which was to be called, East 15 Acting School, under the direction of Margaret Bury. Carol informed me that she would send me two audition pieces and a prospectus.

Well now, that threw me a bit. I had never heard that word before. It's not one we would have used at Cephas Sec Mod, Bethnal Green. Anyway – it arrived along with a date and time for my audition. Monday morning 10.30am, Theatre Royal, E15. Now up to this point, I had never been in a proper theatre, let alone on stage. So, I arrive outside at 10.10am looking into, two large imposing glass doors, trying to build up the courage to enter. I very quickly lost my nerve, and went for a walk around the block, ending up back in front of those doors for a second time.

Once more, my courage deserted me, and I set off once again around that block, in the hope that I would find something inside me, that would push me through those doors, which by now were looking bigger and more imposing than ever. So here I am for the third and last time, standing on the pavement of the Theatre Royal trying my best to find the courage to enter.

Finally, I made up my mind to forget it, go home, and carry on working for British Rail. As I took one step to my right, the Director, Maggie Bury turned the corner and said, "Are you John Lyons?"

I said "Yes."

"Come in," she said, and I was inside before I knew it. I often think about that moment. If I had decided to move three or four seconds before I did, or Maggie had been five or six seconds behind her pace – we would both have passed each other without ever knowing it. I most certainly would never have tried for any other drama school and would never have thought about acting as a profession. I believe an incident like that, is called, sliding doors.

Chapter Nine:
Drama School - The Audition

The audition didn't turn out to be what a normal audition should be. We stood on stage, Maggie and I, and talked about my life and any experience I had in acting. I told her the truth. None at all.

She then suggested I try my two audition pieces, Shakespeare's "Twelfth Night" and a scene from Chekhov's "Three Sisters." Well, again I had to tell her the truth. I couldn't do them because I didn't understand them. With that – she suggested, we forget them and try some improvisations.

Without knowing it, I was playing right into her hands. This was the way theatre workshop actually worked, improvising. Here was a young boy with no pre-conceived ideas on acting. Perfect fodder for what she was looking for. If I had been trying out for any other drama school in the land, I would have very quickly been shown the door. Maggie then suggested a couple of themes for improvising on, and I threw myself into them with ease. So much so, that fifteen minutes later she offered me a place at the school, that would last for the next three years.

Now, I had to go home and tell mum and dad that I am leaving my job, going to drama school, and becoming an actor, with no grant and no money. Well, they understood even less than I did. With myself at British Rail and both my elder sister and brother both bringing money into the house, my mother had finally retired from scrubbing floors. Apparently, my father said to my mother, without me knowing it "Mary, let the boy do it. It might do him a bit of good." I'm glad to say it did. But, my dear mum now had to go back to scrubbing the floors.

Chapter Ten:
Three Years of Drama School

So started the three years that totally changed my life. If I have any education at all, this is where it started. I am now working with people from all over the world – boys and girls who had been to University, Some in their thirties and forties. One or two of them took me under their wings and suggested to me books I should read, plays I should see, films I should watch. One boy, Phillip Hedley, even got his mother Lois, to take me once every three months to Covent Garden to see a Ballet or Opera. This was all to further my education; which of course. I didn't realise at the time.

I took it all in and loved it. It's given me a lifelong interest and enjoyment in classical music, opera and ballet. An expensive hobby, but very rewarding. This was also the time when I obtained my very first passport, so that I could travel with the school to take part in drama festivals in Turkey, and the former state of Yugoslavia. My world was getting bigger. And my mind was expanding, and ready to learn.

With no grant, and parents who could not afford pocket money, I had to find a way of earning extra cash. This turned out to be a blessing in disguise. The school got me a job in the evenings in the professional theatre. I worked every night, covering every job – backstage, stage management, props, even follow spots.

When that theatre was dark, I would go into the big musicals in the West End as a dresser, all the time looking, listening, and learning. So really, I was getting a crash course in theatre. Professional theatre at night, and drama school by day. My other source of income was to meet Ann at the bus stop in Whitechapel Road, she would be going off to work in the City, and I would be going off to drama school. She would, every day, give me two shillings and sixpence in old money for my fare.

So, you can see why we've been married over fifty-five years. I have paid her back since, believe me. Many times over. As the month of March 2015 approached, so did our Golden Wedding. I had asked Ann, a few months previously, how, or where, she would like to spend that very special day. The next day her answer was simple, BEVERLY HILLS, CALIFORNIA. Oh, dear. Well, this would be a once in a lifetime occasion, albeit an expensive one, but let's go for it, and that is what we did.

We flew out five days before the date, with our daughter Laura and her husband Laurence. First stop, The Beverly Hilton Hotel, Wiltshire Boulevard for the first week, which covered our Anniversary. On the special day, we all went for lunch at the Hollywood "Ivy".

The next day, Ann and I moved hotels across town to The Beverly Hills Hotel. This really was showbiz. On the first night, Laura and Laurence joined us for dinner in the hotel's "Polo Lounge" then flew home next morning. Ann and I stayed for another week, doing all the tourist bits that we all do before we flew home. What a wonderful time that was. Expensive? Yes, but well worth It. After all, it was a very special occasion. In a few years' time, it will be our Diamond Anniversary (sixty). So, this time, I think I shall keep my mouth SHUT.

At drama school, we covered almost everything. Dance,

John Lyons

movement, singing, fencing, voice production, which for me was particularly important. When I first started, I had such a strong cockney accent – you could hardly understand a single word I said. One of the teachers, a lovely older actress, by the name of Daphne Heard, offered to come in with me every morning at 9am (the school started at 10am) and she would have a one-to-one lesson with me in elocution.

One of the tricks she had up her sleeve was a peg about three quarters of an inch in length, that she would put between my top and bottom teeth. This had two effects – it made that lazy muscle, that is the tongue, start to work, to come forward and begin to pronounce certain words, plus, it took my voice from my throat, (a common trait in Cockneys) down into my diaphragm. I did this every day for three years - I'm glad to say it worked. Over the course of my career, I've played many parts - Doctors, Solicitors, even Judges – not just Cockney tearaways. Even a PARISH PRIEST. Are you Listening mother? A PARISH PRIEST (she would never believe it).

Chapter Eleven: Going Out Into The Big World of Showbiz

I left drama school in the month of July 1964 at the age of twenty. This was a perfect time to be going into the business. Kitchen sink drama had entered our lives and working class actors were coming more to the fore. Actors like Michael Caine, Alan Bates, Playwrights Arnold Wesker, Harold Pinter, were all writing great parts for actors. Our TV at that time was putting out a stream of dramas, and a lot of one-off plays.

So, there was quite a lot of work to be had. Especially for someone like me, from my background. During the last year of school, casting agents would come down looking for young promising actors for casting in up-coming films. I was lucky enough to be asked along to audition for some very prestigious movies. "Bunny Lake is Missing" with Sir Laurence Olivier, "Modesty Blaise" with Dirk Bogarde, "Poor Cow" for the Director Ken Loach, and "To Sir with Love" to star, Sidney Poitier. I didn't get any of them, but to be given the opportunity, to be thought of in that company, for a boy of nineteen, and with very limited experience, was very encouraging.

In the three weeks leading up to leaving, we, as a school, performed two plays in what is known as a Showcase. In both I was given good parts, and from those I not only gained an agent, (Hamilton and Sydney) with whom I stayed for the next thirty-two years, but also received four different offers of work – of which only two were possible.

John Lyons

I left on a Friday night, and Monday morning I was filming a lead part in an episode of a series called 'Catch Hand' with the actor Anthony Booth for the BBC. Followed by the stage musical 'Oh! What a Lovely War', a Joan Little-wood Production.

With this, I toured not only Great Britain, but all over Europe for the next two years. Taking in France, Belgium, Switzerland and Germany, both East and West. At one stage we played East Berlin for a week, followed by five nights in West Berlin. This proved a big problem, because you were not allowed to take money out of the East, into the West. Which meant that every day for five days, we had to go through "check-point Charlie" twice every day. Can you imagine what the East German Guards were thinking? This was 1964, the Berlin Wall had only been up for four years. What an experience that was.

One of the fascinating things for me was being able to tour all over Europe, with a musical that was set at the time of the First World War. It meant that every third night or so, we would play a theatre, in a Capital City, in a different part of Europe. Every country, Germany, France, Belgium, Holland etc., all had been involved in that war, and all had suffered in very different ways. Which meant that each audience in that particular country, would respond in quite different ways to certain scenes.

For instance, a scene played in a city in Germany, would have a very different response when played in a city in France, and so on. This made each performance, not only different, but fascinating. We never knew what response we would get.

Whilst in West Berlin, the cast attended a drinks party, given by the German State Theatre. I got talking to a young student, who seemed to be something of a local celebrity. After getting to know him a little better, he told me his story. He was born, and had lived his whole life in East Berlin, with his parents and a small dog. For the past four years he had been studying architecture at college but was finding his opportunities limited. What he yearned for was to leave the East, study in the West, and hopefully, travel the world. His parents were fully behind him, wanting him to have a better life.

The Berlin Wall had only been erected one year previously, and the only way to get to the West was to escape. Quite a few East Germans had tried, some successful, others not. If caught, you were imprisoned, or, if seen trying to flee, you could be shot (a little-known fact.)

In the first year of the Wall, those escaping over, or through the Wall, were fired upon, but only a few were killed. The East German Government soon worked out, that the reason for this was that the East German border guards were reluctant to shoot their own countrymen. The solution to this was to pay the border guards a bonus if they shot an escapee. So, escaping could be fatal.

His problem was to find a way to flee, that had not been used before. At the time, while studying at College, he belonged to the Athletic Club, his speciality being the high jump. Of course, there was no way he could jump this large wall, but he could pole vault it. For the next two months he befriended members of the pole vault team, learning the techniques of that sport. The grip on the pole, the upward swing of the body, pushing the pole away etc. plus, at any time, he could borrow a pole to practice for himself.

He told me the first thing he had to do was to find the right place where the border was not so tightly guarded, and at the same time, offer some shelter. This was not easy. He spent many hours on weekends, walking for many miles along the perimeter of the wall, along with his dog, in the hope that anyone noticing him, would take very little notice of a man walking his dog at the weekend.

Once he had found the perfect site, the next job was to work out the distance from the doorway of an empty building where he would start his run, to the base of the wall. This he did by borrowing a camera from the college, the sort that was used in road planning, which also gave him the height of the wall. When he had all this information, the next thing, was practice. For the next three months, on weekends, he would drive out into the countryside, find a secluded spot, and put together a replica of the wall, using string for the top of the wall, and also for the distance he would have to run.

His biggest problem was the pit at the bottom, where the pole is placed before taking off. The only solution was a large, heavy log, which was not ideal, but the best he could come up with. Quite a few times the pole would slip on the grass, but he had to persevere. Come the night that was right - dark, no wind, no moon, he said his goodbyes to his parents, with great sadness, and made his way to his chosen place. Standing in the hidden doorway, with the pole he had left hidden, he waited, and watched a border guard slowly walk along the top of the wall, knowing it would be at least four minutes before he would be back on his return journey.

Dressed only in a T-shirt and sweat pants, he couldn't afford any loose jackets or jumpers that could snag on the top barbed wire that lay across the wall. Once the guard had passed, he gave him one minute to get far enough away, and then, thinking of his parents, went for it. He had calculated he only had ten to twelve seconds to complete his mission, before he would be spotted, and maybe, shot. The dash across the empty ground went well, the placing of the pole at the base of the wall was good (that was the part that worried him most). Then the last bit was the upward swing which would take him over the wall. Perfect.

Not Just George

The only piece of the jigsaw missing, was, what was on the other side where he would land? The night had gone so well so far, it couldn't end here. It didn't. The other side was all grass. On landing, he fell awkwardly, twisted his back, but was still able to stand and hobble twenty or so yards to safety, where he finally sunk to the floor in relief, and cried. What a story. Now, I may have added a few bits myself, but that is basically his story. And a true one. If it isn't, he was a very good actor.

This musical, "Oh! What a Lovely War," is where I first met, and shared digs with my dear friend Nigel Hawthorne (later Sir Nigel). He was in fact a guest at our wedding in the East End in 1965.

Let me just give you a quick insight into the sort of person Nigel was. He had come over from South Africa many years earlier, in the hope of finding good acting jobs in England. At the time he lived with his then partner in a small flat in Maida Vale. Every Christmas morning, Ann and I would go over, along with just a few other people for drinks.

When twelve o'clock came round, we all left to go home to our own festivities, but both Nigel and his partner would go to the local Old Peoples home, and there, serve lunch for the next couple of hours to the old folks. They did this for many years. A small thing to do perhaps, but none the least, it showed the kind of person he was, and how he thought about other people.

A man with a very warm heart, but unfortunately, that heart let him down on Boxing Day, 2001. A sad day. If you re-member, Sir Nigel had great success playing "King George III" at the National Theatre. He then went on to play the same part in a major film adaptation, for which he was nominated in the category of best actor, at the Oscars. He later told me a funny little story about this. When he was taken over to Hollywood to attend the ceremony, part of the deal was to make a two-week tour of America, the purpose being to promote the film. At the first stop, he noticed that the title for the film had been changed to just, "The Madness of King George"

When he asked where the numbers III had gone? The reply was, "If we had called it "The Madness of King George III" the American audiences would think they had missed parts one and two. I'm inclined to believe that, what about you?

A very strange and unusual happening occurred during this tour. We had just completed a four-night run in Vienna and left for Zurich the next day. After checking into our designated hotels and making our way to the theatre in the afternoon, the Company Manager confronted us all with the news that of the two trucks carrying all the costume and props, one of them had gone off the road in the snow, and was now in a ditch somewhere between Zurich and Vienna.

A meeting was called, and it was decided that the show would go on that night come what may. Well, off we all go down into the theatre's costume and props department to find anything that could be used in a song or a sketch. For the next hour we all chipped in with ideas and musical numbers. The curtain went up at seven, but not before our Company Manager, Owen Teale, had made an announcement, explaining the problem to a full house.

Away we went. Things were going far better than anyone had expected when the Stage Manager walked onto the stage and announced that the two trucks had finally arrived. He followed this by inviting the whole audience to return for a midnight performance, if possible. This brought about a standing ovation. By now the audience were well and truly on our side.

Not Just George

Off they went, some to make phone calls for baby-sitters, others to make a quick trip home, if they lived close enough, for refreshments. Come midnight, all were back in their seats in great anticipation. The curtain rose to a ten minute ovation even before a word or a song had been uttered. By two thirty when the curtain finally fell, we couldn't leave the stage for at least another half hour, because of so many people wanting to come forward to shake hands and take photos.

By this time of course, all the local newspapers had been notified, which meant that by the next day the whole event, plus photographs, appeared in many English newspapers. We were described as heroes. I'm not too sure about that.

Also, it was during the European leg of that tour when Ann popped the question. We had reached the city of Zurich in Switzerland from where I had arranged to call Ann back in London at seven-thirty London time. Of course, this had to be done via phone boxes, as neither of us had phones at home.

All was going well when I noticed the money was running out. That's when she made her move. Together with my mum, they had picked a day and a church where we could be married.

I looked again at the money situation, which was almost up. Well, I had little choice but to say, "Yes." I would of course have popped the question myself when I got home, but she got in first. When Ann and my mother went to meet the Vicar to call the banns, the Vicar asked Ann, "Where is the intended groom?"

Quite innocently she replied, "At the moment he's away, but he will be home in four weeks."

After the wedding, the Vicar told me, in confidence, that he thought I was serving a term in prison. On the day of our wedding, we of course hired a professional photographer. He duly turned up at the reception in the evening with the proofs of the photos he had taken during the day. With the word "proof" written across them (remember this was the mid-sixties) for all friends and relatives to place orders.

We never saw him again. He never came back, never called, just disappeared. We never did find out what the problem was. Consequently, the only two photographs we have at home of the wedding, is one of Ann and I on the church steps. As with the passing of time, those photos have got old, yellow, and cracked. And the letter "R" has faded, so, when you look at them, running right down my body from top to bottom, is the word "POOF". What a great wedding present.

The next day, Ann, and her three bridesmaids, had to get all dressed up again, go up to the roof of the block of flats she was living in at the time, and have photographs taken again, by her uncle using an old box Kodak. Very glam.

If you remember when I first entered drama school, I had no idea what I was getting myself into, or even if I wanted to be an actor. Now, after three years, I most certainly did. Now I had found something I could do, something I could be quite good at, and maybe something I could make a career out of. I do remember saying to Ann at the time: "Wouldn't it be a wonderful life, if I could still be doing this in fifty years?" Well, it's now been fifty-nine years and I'm still working. And it has been a wonderful life.

Chapter Twelve:
A Long and Varied Career

As I have said, my very first job on leaving drama school was the lead in an episode of a series called "Catch Hand". Back in the sixties at drama school, we were trained for the theatre, not TV or Film. Now, all drama schools have courses in film technique, with cameras on site, so that students can work with them under the supervision of visiting professional directors and cameramen. I had none of that.

On my first day filming for the BBC, I just had to learn on my feet. One thing I had going for me was the ability to ask questions. I quickly found out that people were very happy to pass on their knowledge to a newcomer, if you approached them in the right way. I then, as I said, went straight into the Joan Littlewood Production of "Oh! What a Lovely War". Whilst on my last six months of drama school, I worked on this production at Stratford East, backstage, when Joan, and her producer Gerry Raffles asked me to join the Company when the time came for me to leave.

I jumped at the chance. What a great show that was. All set around the First World War, in which all of us actors played at least eight different parts. (A quick insight as to how Ms Littlewood worked). Six months into the tour, we were playing the Theatre Royal Nottingham. Joan had not seen the show for at least six months and came up on the Monday night. After that night's performance, our Stage

Manager put out the call for the next day's notes. Two-thirty on stage.

When we all arrived next day, Joan was sitting in the middle of the stage with a face like thunder. She then promptly tore into the previous night's performance. How we were all taking it for granted, walking through the show, no one listening to the other actor, and so on. She then held up a list of cast changes for that night's performance. We were all going to change roles where possible. "Raymond, you will play all John's parts, Rio, you will play all Kent's parts" and so on.

Well, everybody fell silent with shock. "She can't mean this."

"It's Joan Littlewood, she does."

We all then frantically began running around collecting the other actors' props and bits of costume, asking silly questions like "Where do you come on from?"

"What do you wear in that scene?" etc., out of sheer panic.

Of course, we all went on that night with Joan out front. The next day at notes, she loved it, thought it was the best she had ever seen it. Suddenly we were all listening to each other again, everyone was back on their toes, life was back into the production. The next night we all returned to our own original parts, but the lesson had been learnt. "Oh! What a Lovely Woman".

Whilst on tour in Austria, another actor who had been in the business for quite a few years, suggested to me a little professional trick for getting work when the tour had finished, and we got back to England. It involved going to a photography studio and having some head shots taken of me. We then bought air mail envelopes, and posted as many as we could think of, along with a covering letter and the head shot, to casting agents and producers back home. The idea being, that when these air mail envelopes arrived on the person's desk, with Austrian stamps emblazoned on the front, they would go straight to the top of the pile. Which they did.

So, thanks to my dear long-time friend Kent Baker, I got quite a few jobs over the years from that little ruse. Back home in London, and married, work became a little slow. One day, I got a call from a student friend from drama school, who at this time between jobs, was running the stage management side of a strip club in London's Soho. (Lady Jane Grey's). It only needed two people to run the show, so if I would join them, one person would always be free if an audition came up. Perfect.

Each show lasted one hour, but there were twelve shows a day. A long day. Twelve noon to twelve midnight. The job entailed changing the sets between acts, setting the lighting, music cues etc. What I wasn't informed about was the little matter of, putting on full costume, and going on with one of the girls during her act.

This, when it was my turn, was to play King Charles, entering on stage with a large bunch of flowers, present them to Nell Gwyn, then sit on a chair while Nell slowly removed all her clothes in gratitude. Not too difficult. Not after three years in drama school. But, for the other entrance, I was required to put on a full Batman costume, and whilst the girl on stage was pretending to be asleep and dreaming, I would enter through the French windows, stand on a very small multi coloured revolve and pose.

She would then spend the next ten minutes dancing around the man of her dreams. For me, this was a nightmare. On the nights when there was a big football match taking place at Wembley, and all the drunken supporters hit Soho for a night out, can you imagine what I went through? Oh, my.

John Lyons

One of the perks of the job was this: after a few weeks, and the girls had got to know me, one of them asked me if I would kindly apply some body make up across her back. Two days later she asked if I would kindly do the back of her legs as well. (I'm sure you can see where I'm going). Oh yes, by the end of the week she had turned around, and I was doing the Full Monty.

I did such a good job, that by the end of the month I had another client, one of the older girls. Of course, as we all know, all good things must come to an end. This little painting and decorating job did as well when my agent got me an audition at the BBC, for a part in a TV series called "UNITED".

This was one of the first soaps to be put out twice a week by the BBC in the sixties. I got the job, and signed a contract for six months, with another six months option, to play the part of Alan Murdoch. The show was recorded in a studio in Birmingham, which meant that Ann and I had to move full time up to Brum. We were very lucky to move into a lovely big flat, with a big garden, that had been occupied just recently by that wonderful actor Albert Finney, whilst he had been a member of the Birmingham Rep Company, and before moving on to greater things.

Working on a TV series that put out two thirty-minute episodes a week in five days, meant you had to learn very quickly. Which I did. It was great training for a young actor. On at least two occasions when the writers found they were running five minutes or so under, dialogue had to be quickly written and given to the actors on the spot.

On occasions when this fell to me, and it was a two shot with another actor, my script had to be pinned to his chest, and his to mine. Which meant, when he had a close up, I could take a quick look at my dialogue, and likewise for him. I couldn't do that today.

Not Just George

Being in a series which was based around a football team, we of course had a side made up from the actors in the show. We played many charity matches whenever possible, and trained and filmed each Sunday of the month, for the football sequences to be slotted into each episode. These were filmed at Coventry City's training ground. All this came about through Coventry's Manager at the time, Jimmy Hill. Jimmy himself had been a professional footballer with Fulham, and a future chairman of the Football Association. Jimmy was also the script advisor on the series, which meant we all got to know him pretty well.

He once said a very strange, but nice thing to me after one particular charity football match. Whilst having dinner, he looked across the table and said, "Lad, if I had got you when you were fifteen, I could have made a professional player out of you."

I'm not sure if he could have, but it wouldn't have lasted for fifty-eight years. When the series was running on TV it would be watched by many professional players, simply because it was set around a football team. At least twice a week, a few members of the cast would have a night out at one of Birmingham's top Nightclubs, THE CEDAR CLUB. One particular night, West Ham Football Club had been playing Birmingham, and were now in the Club. There was the great Jimmy Greaves, Martin Peters, and Geoff Hurst.

After a little while, Geoff Hurst made his way over, stood next to me and said, "Could I possibly have your autograph?" This shook me. I looked at him for a moment, and then replied, "Three months ago, you scored three goals in a World Cup Final, and you want MY autograph?" What a moment to treasure. I met Mr Hurst a year ago, at a function, and reminded him of that moment nearly fifty years ago, he couldn't remember. So much for fame.

John Lyons

When, in 1967 the series was taken off, and replaced by 'Z Cars', I went straight back into Joan Littlewood's Company at Stratford East. For the next two years we did various plays, ranging from restoration comedies, to modern American. One play was a very funny musical called "Macbird". In this again I played many parts, as we all did. At the time I shared a dressing room with the actor Jimmy Perry. Jimmy had in our dressing room an old Remington typewriter, on which he would bang away all day, and every day.

Finally, one afternoon, I had had enough. I had to ask him what he was up to, "Jim, you're driving me mad with that typewriter, what are you writing?"

"Oh, it's just an idea I have about the Home Guard." A few years later, he presented it to David Croft at the BBC, and it became "DAD'S ARMY" I never did get a part. Shame, It's a great show.

One of the many productions I did do was, a production of "Mrs Wilson's Diary". This was taken from a long running series published monthly in "Private Eye" and turned into a musical by Joan, written by John Wells and Richard Ingram, based of course around all the shenanigans going on in Harold Wilson's Government at the time.

We ran for five weeks at Stratford East, to quite a lot of interest from West End managements. Finally, the production was offered a West End run at the Criterion Theatre in Piccadilly Circus (another interesting insight into the working mind of Ms Littlewood). It was the last night of the run at Stratford East, before opening on the Monday at the Criterion. I'm sharing a dressing room with two long serving members of the Company, Bob Grant and Stephen Lewis, who both went on to appear, and on occasions write "On the Buses." Everything was going as normal when we reached the interval, and the three of us were back in the dressing room.

Not Just George

Suddenly the dressing room door flew open, and Ms Little-wood entered. Straight away she flew into a rage, all direct-ed at me. "John Lyons, what were you doing on that stage tonight? That's the worst performance I've seen all year."

She went on like this for the next five minutes, with quite a few choice words thrown in, threw the script on the floor, and made a rather over the top grand exit, slamming the door behind her. Well, Stephen, Bob and I, looked at each other in amazement. Finally, Stephen, who had known Joan for many years said, "There's something more to that."

That something turned out to be this. At the end of the last night's performance, I was making my way across the stage, heading for the bar, when Joan's Manager and partner Gerry Raffles, stopped me and asked, "What's the problem John? Joan tells me you don't want to go into town with the show."

"Gerry, I never said such a thing" I replied. He looked at me, and then gave me that lovely warm smile of his.

"Don't worry boy, I'll sort it out."

I learnt a couple of months later, what it was all about. She, Joan, on the following Monday morning was starting rehearsals on a new musical, "The Marie LIoyd Story" with Avis Bunnage and Nigel Hawthorne. It appears there were five different characters in this play that she wanted me for.

But instead of asking me, we went through this whole farce in the dressing room, so that I would leave "Mrs Wilson" and put myself out of work. The idea, apparently being, she would have called during that week and said something to the effect of, "Come on in you silly sod, I'll find a few parts in this for you" therefore maintaining the upper hand. That's all I can think of. What a strange way to work.

Well, I didn't want to play that daft game and miss out on
my first West End debut, so I did open on the Monday night
at the Criterion Theatre, where we stayed for the next two
years. One of the great benefits of being in a production
like this was that as members of the Government changed,
so did we. For instance, When George Brown was sacked,
he was replaced by Roy Jenkins (played once again with
great charm by my dear Nigel Hawthorne) which meant we
all picked up different parts to play, which kept it fresh and
interesting. It helps greatly in a long run.

One of the many incidents that happened during this long
run, involved Bob Grant. Bob and I, along with our other
roles, played two removal men, who enter in the last scene
of the first act, to move Mrs Wilson from number 10, to
number 11. The show had been running now for over a
year, and actors were getting tired and complacent. One
mid-week matinee, I'm standing by the doorway, waiting
for our cue to enter, when the stage manager and myself
notice, no Mr Grant. He has fallen asleep in our dressing
room.

The cue comes, Mrs Wilson comes to the door to answer it,
when, I feel the hand of the stage manager in the middle of
my back, and I'm pushed on. Everyone looks, and we go
into the dialogue for the scene. All the while, we can hear
Bob running as fast as he can, down the very long corridor of the Criterion Theatre, swearing as he goes. When
he enters, out of breath, he pulls his flat cap over his head,
and then proceeds with sign language, as if he is deaf and
dumb. He doesn't know a word. I now have to play both
parts. The Devil.

The scene is going rather well, I seem to be remember-
ing both parts, when it suddenly dawns on me, there is a
big song and dance number that finished the act, and I (as
Bob's character) start the whole thing off. Well, I'm not too

bad when it comes to singing in shows, but it is hit or miss if I can hit that first note cleanly. If I don't, it's possible a few people will follow me, and the whole number will be a mess.

The dialogue ends, the small band strikes up, I take a deep breath, and hit a perfect note that Pavarotti would have been proud of. Job done. When we got off, he apologised, and said "John, I owe you one." He did keep his word a couple of years later, when he asked me if I wanted to take over from him in a West End production of Paul Raymond's "Pyjama Tops."

He did get me a comp to go and see it, I thanked him, but said "No thanks Bob" it wasn't my thing. He understood. Years later when he was writing some of the scripts for "On the Buses" along with Stephen Lewis, he would always write a part for me. A very sad day when he passed away.

The TV executive and television personality David Frost came along to see the show on quite a few occasions. He, being associated with both Richard Ingram and John Wells, offered to have the show filmed for television, which indeed we did, over two separate Sundays whilst the show was still running in the West End.

It was to be filmed at LWT (London Weekend Television) studios in Wembley. The director was to be Stuart Allen. Stuart, while directing the show was also in the middle of planning and getting together a new television series to be called "On the Buses" as a vehicle for Reg Varney, written by Chesney and Wolfe. The rest of the characters for that show had yet to be cast, but by the end of filming "Mrs Wilson", Stuart had decided to offer the part of the Inspector to Stephen, and the part of Jack the conductor alongside Reg, to Bob Grant. He also very kindly offered me a minor role that would feature in quite a few episodes.

Unfortunately for me, during the first week's rehearsal, Stuart and the writers thought that the cast was getting over loaded, which meant my small character had to be dropped. It was a blow, but dear Stuart very kindly said, that "if at any time you need work, get your agent to call and I'll find something for you."

He was true to his word. For over the six or eight years I appeared in six episodes of "On the Buses," at one point taking over from Reg, who had fallen ill that particular week. Meeting and getting to know and work with Stuart Allen proved to be very beneficial to me. Not only "On the Buses" but he asked for me many times in different comedies he was directing for both London Weekend, and Thames Television. Series such as "Mind Your Language", "Love Thy Neighbour", "Never Mind the Quality, Feel the Width" and many more.

This sort of work on TV got me noticed by other producers/ directors, they saw in me an ability for comedy. Peter Fraser-Jones asked for me for an episode of "George and Mildred" (starring my old friends Brian Murphy and Yootha Joyce, both I had worked with many times at Stratford East). Over the years I appeared in four episodes of that show playing a different character every time.

When rehearsing one particular episode of a series called "Public Eye" at the Thames Studio in Twickenham, I went up to the bar at lunchtime. What a fortunate stroke of luck this turned out to be. For there I met producer/director William G Stewart. Bill was one of the top producers at Thames and offered me a part in a series he was directing at that precise time.

He came over, introduced himself and said "You're John Lyons, aren't you? John, you haven't worked for me before, but I do know your work. I've got a small part in the next episode I'm directing, it's only one scene, but if you want it, it's yours." What a slice of good fortune this turned out to be.

Over the next twenty or so years, I went on to work for Bill at least another fifty times. Not all comedies, but mostly. He put me in shows such as "Man About the House", "Tickets for the Titanic", "Doctor in the House", and the "Harry Worth Show". At that time, the writer Johnny Speight had written a series of sketches which Bill was about to direct. Johnny Speight had of course, had a big hit at the BBC with "Till Death Do Us Part". He then joined up with another top comedy writer Ray Galton. Ray's writing credits were long and illustrious. Along with Alan Simpson they wrote "Hancock's Half Hour", "Steptoe and Son", to name only two.

They got together and wrote the first seven episodes based on a fictitious police station, in a London suburb, called Woodley. In the cast were actors of the calibre such as Norman Rossington, Dermot Kelly, myself and Peter Cleall. The lead character was to be played by Ronald Fraser, a face and talent that graced the screens both in film and TV for many years. Ronnie's face once seen, never forgotten. The name of the series was "Spooner's Patch".

We filmed the first seven episodes at the ATV studios in Elstree. The very first episodes were due to go out to air on a Monday night at eight o'clock in the evening, following Coronation Street, prime time viewing. This couldn't have been better. At seven o'clock that same night, ATV workers and technicians pulled the plugs, and went out on strike. This strike lasted for quite a few weeks, so when transmission was resumed, all the schedules were changed, which meant our very first episode went out at eleven o'clock at night.

That's how it went on, the kiss of death. It never recovered. But, undaunted, Bill, Johnny and Ray were determined to carry on. Unfortunately, by then we had lost Ronnie Fraser and Norman Rossington to other commitments. Which meant that they had to recast the part of Inspector Spooner. The lead part went to that very fine actor and writer Donald Churchill, and in a stroke of genius they created a part of a female traffic warden to be played by veteran actress Patricia Hayes. Many people would remember Pat not only for her many comedy performances on TV and radio, but her prize-winning performance as "Edna the Inebriated Woman" for which she won a BAFTA. "Spooner" became great fun to be part of, but unfortunately it never did recover from that bad stroke of luck at the beginning, and after completing twenty-one episodes, it sadly came to an end.

Before the last episode had been finished, Ann and I, with our daughter, who at this time was still in arms, paid a visit to my mum's flat in Limehouse. When we left, our quickest way home was straight down WHITE HORSE LANE. Halfway down, we go around a sharp bend, and there in the middle of the road, is standing a very large WHITE HORSE. Now, I know this sounds a bit farfetched, and too much of a coincidence, but it's true.

I pull over to the side of the road, tell my wife to stay where she is, and get out of the car. This great big white horse, just stands still and looks at me, unafraid, as if used to being around people. Around its neck is a long piece of rope, which he is very happy for me to pick up. Now, I have to think what to do with this lovely animal. I can't go home and leave it standing in the middle of the road on a dark November night, I wouldn't be able to sleep.

From the car, Ann shouts out, "Arbour Square Police Station."

"Good thinking girl, it's five minutes away, lock the door, I won't be long."

Off I go, with the horse very happily following on behind. When I reach the police station, it's obvious I can't take him in, so, like Clint Eastwood, I tie him up to the railings outside. Being on TV every Monday night playing a policeman, as I approach the counter, the young police constable on duty, gives me that strange look that says, "I've seen you somewhere before."

"Now Constable," says I "You're not going to believe this, but I have just tied a large white horse up to your railings outside."

He didn`t say anything, he just looked.

"Believe me, I'm not kidding, you have to come and see for yourself. " I didn't blame him, he called back into the rear office for the Sergeant to accompany him. After all, he could have been stepping outside with the Mad Axeman.

Once they had seen the situation, and realised I wasn't kidding, they took over. Luckily that particular Station had horse stables at the rear, so my horse would at least be safe for the night. Finally, the penny dropped for both of them.

"You're an actor, aren't you?"

"Yes I am."

"You're in that police comedy about a police station on Monday nights."

"That's right." We do another five minutes chat, and I excuse myself, knowing my wife and daughter are waiting for me back at the car. When at home, we sit down with a glass of wine, and figure out how this could have happened.

Ann comes up with the answer. "Five or so streets away from White Horse Lane, is a children's farm, Stepping Stones, they have many types of animals, including horses. That's where it must have wandered out from."

"Yes of course, that has to be the answer."

Next day I'm at the ATV Studios in Borehamwood for rehearsals of "Spooner's Patch".

As I arrive, the first thing the floor manager says is, "You had a busy weekend"

"What do you mean?"

"Your friend, the white horse."

"How do you know about that?"

"It`s in the newspapers". Sure enough it was, plus a small photo of me. The only way this could have happened was information from the police station, who do pass on tit bits to newspapers, in return for any info they, the newspapers, can put their way. So, next time you find yourselves in a police station, keep your wits about you.

Both Bill, and Johnny Speight had not forgotten me. Johnny started to write a series for the great Eric Sykes based around a golf club to be called "The 19th Hole›, which is the bar of a golf club. I was cast as one of the members of the Club.

I had worked once before with Eric in an episode of his long running series on BBC TV – "Sykes" and he remembered me. I greatly admired Eric and we got on very well together. I did enjoy watching him work, always inventing, always looking for pieces of comedy biz to use. I may have enjoyed it, but not all the other actors did. Especially those that just came in for one episode and found that when their character had a fairly long speech, Eric would be inventing a bit of business in the background. It didn't cause any real problems, and the live audience in the studio loved it.

Unfortunately, the other actors were not very happy about it. In truth, I can understand. We went on and finished seven episodes of that particular series, up at Central TV, and that was due to be the end of it. Mr Speight, Bill and Eric had other ideas. Johnny wrote a stage play using all the same characters. I was cast in my original role and a date was set for the opening of a three-month tour of the country. Ten days before rehearsals were about to being, the production company, taking it out on tour, were offered another theatre where the play could start the tour.

For me, this was unfortunate. It meant that it would open one week earlier than originally planned, and at that time I was filming a true crime play for LWT and wouldn't have been available for that week. So, I missed out on a job I was greatly looking forward to. Not only watching and working with the great Mr Sykes, but also spending some time with him on tour. One of the few disappointments in my working life. A wonderful, warm man.

Chapter Thirteen:
Ridley and Me

You may have noticed that throughout my career I worked most of the time. Which is most unusual for actors. One of the reasons for this is I accepted almost all of the acting jobs I was offered. This would bring me into contact with many directors and casting agents, who once they had used me and were happy with my work, would think of me for many other projects.

This also worked for me in the advertising world of TV commercials. Over the years I have probably been in fifty-five commercials at the last count. The first was a big one back in the late 60s. The director Ridley Scott. Not bad eh! Of course, Ridley was not one of the foremost Hollywood film directors he is today, but everyone at that time could see that this man was heading for bigger things. His talent shone out.

At the time I met Ridley, he was filming at least three or four commercials in one week, so for him, time was of the utmost, it couldn't be wasted. The first commercial I did was for Hovis flour, which we filmed in a small studio in Soho, London. I got on very well with Ridley, well I must have done as he went on to use me in another twenty or so more commercials. He would say "Get me John Lyons - he'll fit that."

I found out why I was used so much on a lunchtime break I spent with his manager. He told me Ridley was so busy with every aspect of filming, lighting, cameras, and the product itself, that time could not be wasted worrying about the artist. So, when he found people that he not only liked and trusted, and would give him a quick and professional job, even if he had given you directions at eight o'clock in the morning and you weren't used until maybe four o'clock that afternoon, you hadn't forgotten, fallen asleep, or God forbid got drunk. In other words, a good professional job.

I had become one of Ridley Scott's Repertory Company. I advertised everything from soap to petrol, yoghurt to car wax. This brought me to the attention of other TV commercial directors. Bernie Stringle for one, who again used me quite a few times. I do remember doing the KFC Funky Chicken walk, down the Bayswater Road, with my lovely friends Toni Palmer and Brian Hall (who went on to play Terry the chef in "Fawlty Towers"). All three of us tried our hardest to hide our faces away from the camera in that one, hoping not to be seen.

A lot of actors around that time would not do commercials, they were above it, but I found them a means to an end. Not only did they bring me into contact with new casting agents, who, as time passed, went on to cast bigger things than just commercials. But if you were lucky, commercials could generate a substantial sum of money which would enable you to work in Fringe Theatre, where you got paid no money at all, or just expenses.

Fringe Theatre was great fun and would give you the chance to play parts that you would not normally be cast for, plus the chance to find out things you didn't even think you could do. With also, I'm glad to say, very little pressure. After all, you were working for nothing. For me, one of the parts that has given me the greatest satisfaction, was working in a Fringe Theatre (The Bridewell Theatre in Fleet Street). This was a production of a long-lost Ameri-

John Lyons

can Musical "PURLEY" set in the deep south of America during the 1800s. The part I was asked to play, was the Landowner, with a deep Southern accent.

Apart from the young boy who played my son, the rest of the cast were Black Americans. We were the only white actors in the play. This was going to be a big challenge for me, what with the Southern accent to get right, alongside all the other authentic accents around me. I worked very hard on this, and was very pleased and gratified when members of the cast gave me encouraging comments on my accent.

This musical had not been produced for many years, certainly not over here. It's a great shame. It really is a fine show, with great songs. I myself only had one song within it, but the singing from other members of the cast was of the highest level. Made the hairs stand up on the back of the neck. This whole production was wonderfully directed by Omar Okai. It showed me one or two things that I never thought I was capable of. The benefits of working in Fringe.

It was also a very good shop window to be seen in, as all were based in Central London. Most plays ran for about one hour or so, which allowed casting people to pop in during their lunch break. One play I did at the Soho Poly was seen by the director Glen Walford, and the manager of the "Belgrade Theatre" Coventry. Out of that, I got a six-month contract to appear at the Belgrade in three different plays. It always amazed me how one job could lead to another.

From being seen in commercials and having my photograph in Spotlight (a yearly book, with the photos and info on actors and actresses widely used by casting agents) I was approached by a very prominent photographer, Michael Joseph. Michael had done some great work in the

Sixties and Seventies, especially with the Rolling Stones and booked me for a photographic season at his studio based in Holborn London, for a soft drinks campaign.

The reason Michael wanted to use me, was not because I was the handsome male model type, but that my face, he told me had "a lot of character and warmth." Plus, actors were more animated and less inhibited than most models. Over the years I went on to do many photographic shoots for Michael. Paint, Debenhams Clothing, and so on.

One product in particular, nearly brought an end to my career on two occasions. This was a campaign for German cigarettes, to be shown both on German TV, and appear in German Magazines. We were filming at Bodiam Castle in Sussex, a most beautiful location. I'm sitting in a small rowing boat, in the middle of the moat that surrounds the Castle. Imagine this. I'm dressed as a deep-sea diver, in full costume, apart from the big diver's boots, which were on show behind me. The crew are situated on the other side of the moat, on the bank, ready for action.

My instructions were, to put on the big and heavy helmet, lock it in place at the last minute, and, on action, jump into the air from the boat, into the moat, which wasn't very deep, probably up to my waist. Good. I put on the diver's helmet and locked it into place and waited for my cue to jump.

Suddenly, and thank heavens he did, a passer-by walking his dog, said to our director, Michael Joseph "Is that man about to jump into that moat?"

"Yes, he is" replied Michael.

"Don`t you realise, without his heavy boots on, he will be top heavy, and as soon as he hits the water, he will turn upside down and will probably drown before you can reach him?"

"My word", (or words to that effect) said Michael. "John. Stop. You must put your boots on."

I can see, two big heavy assistants row out, take off my helmet, and help me put on those big and heavy boots. Last of all they replace the diver's helmet, which has been doctored, so that all openings would now not let in any water. Back they go to land. Now, we are ready to go. I get the thumbs up, and the white flag which means action. I jump up, as far as my weight will let me, and land perfectly on my feet in the moat, with my head and shoulders out of the water. Perfect, came the hand signals from the shore.

I can't hear a thing, because all the holes of the helmet have been closed up tight. But I can see the two big heavy assistants rowing back out to help me. By the time they reach me, I'm already misting up inside. The first thing they have to do is remove the big and heavy helmet, so that I can get air.

This now is proving a bit of a problem. When they put it on me, they locked it far too tight, and now it would not budge. I could just about see them through the mist, signalling back to base that there was a problem. By now, it's been quite a few minutes, and not only is the eyepiece misting up, but I could hear my own breathing, and it was getting LOUDER. It's strange what thoughts go through your mind at times of stress and panic.

For me, I grabbed the large diver's knife that was part of the costume, and tried to stab myself, in the hope of letting in some air. What a fool. Thank heavens, on the third thrust of the knife, the helmet suddenly came free, and air rushed back into my lungs. Not only to my great relief, but to all back on shore.

Three months later, I hadn't learnt my lesson. For the same product, German cigarettes, I found myself on top of a

Stately Home, in full flowing costume, waiting for a delivery, by helicopter, of the German cigarettes, which would then be deposited down into the attic window of the house. Not a very clever idea.

The director was situated, along with his cameraman, and assistant, on a large crane, which would follow both me and the helicopter. As luck would have it, the weather took a turn for the worse. Heavy rain all day. A decision had to be made. This shoot was now proving to be very expensive, what with the crew, hire of the Stately Home, the helicopter, and last of all, ME, the artist. The decision was made to go with the weather.

Because of the very expensive costume I was wearing, and the heavy rain, I was given an extra-large umbrella. Okay... off we go for a take. I'm now on the top of the slated roof, standing next to the attic window, guiding the helicopter in. Now, nobody thought of this, including myself, but as the chopper got closer to me, the under draft from the chopper's rotating blades got hold of me, and suddenly I became Mary Poppins, flying through the air. With great fortune, I was able to drop the umbrella, grab hold of the chimney stack, and stay there until the helicopter moved away. I don't need to tell you, that was the end of my adventures with German cigarettes.

The advertising world in the seventies and eighties, seemed to be a law unto themselves. Quite a few advertising companies from around the world would come over to London, not only for our large range of actors, of all ages, but directors, and creative personnel. Plus, a week in swinging London on an expense account, must have been very tempting. And at that time, money seemed to be no object.

For instance. I was asked to go along to audition for Kodak Instant cameras, to be shown only on French Television. I got the job. I couldn't understand why, the part being a

French husband, taking instant snaps of his two children. I'm sure they could have found a more French looking dad than me back home, but there you go. The part entailed dad having a broken arm, showing that this camera could easily be operated with one hand.

So, come the day, they fly me over to Paris, I'm picked up at the airport, and driven to a studio in the centre of Paris, where I'm measured up for a plaster cast, and wardrobe, then put back on the plane, with instructions to be back in two weeks time, for two days filming. What a lovely job.

It got better. I fly out two weeks later, get taken to a nice hotel, then given three days expenses for meals in the evening. Once those two days filming were completed, and I had spent two nights exploring the centre of Paris, and eating rather well, I was again put on a plane, with thanks for a job well done.

A week passes, when my agent gets a call asking if John could come back to Paris the next day, to re-shoot the commercial?

Of course, he could, but the fee would have to increase slightly. The reason for this re-shoot was, the next day, when the film would have been developed, it was noticed that the two French children playing the kids, had put their hands across my face at just the wrong time (this would not happen today, we now have instant playback in cameras, which shows any mistakes that have taken place) In the seventies you had to send the film to be developed overnight.

Off I fly once more. Again, a nice hotel, expenses, plus two days filming, and back home. Can you see where this is going? YES... the kids had done it again. Back I go for a third time. Same script. One month goes by, and once more the call comes. "Could John return just one more time?"

Not Just George

This time it wasn't the kids but a technical problem. Every time, my fee, plus expenses, are going upwards. By the time I'm met at the airport by the producer, this, including the plaster cast and wardrobe call, is my fifth visit. He greets me, hugs me warmly, (by now we are old friends) and he says "John, I think it would be cheaper to buy you an apartment in Paris". What a job. If I ever have a problem finding acting work, I'm sure I could become a tour guide in Gay Paree.

Time passes, and the same casting agent puts me up for a commercial for Spanish Television, to be filmed in Barcelona over three days, advertising Hotpoint Fridges. Again, this Englishman from London is cast as a Spanish salesman. (I told you they were a law unto themselves). Off I go to lovely Barcelona, but this time, there's a catch. I have to learn the script in Spanish and talk straight into camera.

Wouldn't it again have been easier and far cheaper to hire a Spanish actor? Because no matter how good, or bad my Spanish was, it was always going to be dubbed by a Spanish actor in the end. All they wanted was for my mouth to make the right shapes. Crazy. It wasn't easy, but I did it, and they seemed happy. Now comes payment time. It had been agreed between my Agent and the Spanish production company, that I would be paid on completion of the job in cash. I have forgotten the reason, but at the time I think it was legal.

I signed the release form, and the secretary duly paid me out in Spanish Pesetas. Now, at the time, I can't remember how many Pesetas there were to the pound, but it was a lot. I mean thousands. I had my plane ticket in my bag, and off I go to the airport and check in. Just as I'm passing through the gate, two bearded custom officers stop me and ask if they can look in my bag. In there, they of course find a rather large bundle of Spanish pesetas. Communication at

70

this time is not easy, but I think I'm being asked to empty my pockets onto the counter.

Now there is money coming out of everywhere, coat, wallet, trouser pocket, everywhere. I think I'm being asked now to explain, what I'm doing in Spain, and why am I taking so much money out of the country? Luckily, I found in my wallet the name and number of the company I have just been working for. Good. They now start making phone calls. Over the loudspeaker, they are calling for the last passengers on the flight to London. I'm trying my best to remain calm but take off is getting close.

Then, just before the gates are closing, one officer puts the phone down, and gestures for me to quickly, gather my pesetas, and go quickly through the gate. I got into my seat with about ten minutes to spare and let out a sigh of relief.

That night, at home, I'm explaining my ordeal to my wife, while at the same time counting the Spanish pesetas, of which I shall pass on ten per cent to my agent. Between us, we must have counted that money five times, and worked out what should have been the equivalent in pounds. You know what I'm going to say, don't you? I only have half the money I had when I first arrived at that airport. There is no way I could prove it, but you wouldn't have to be JACK FROST to work it out.

One commercial that could have changed the course of my acting career was the Kellogg's brand. At the time I was just finishing the third year of "Frost" when I went up for the casting of a series of commercials for all Kellogg's products. The part I was there for was, "Mr K". The head of the "K Family" The idea for this campaign was to follow on where the 'Oxo family' had finished. If you remember that campaign ran on our TV for years. I got the job. For the first time in my life, I was hoping not to get it, knowing that if I did, being a long running and high profile campaign, I would have to pull out of "Frost" plus any other TV work that could have come my way. One of the reasons being, if you were appearing in a programme on TV, a commercial that you were in, could not be shown in its advertising breaks.

For that reason alone, you were going to be paid very, very well, seeing as you would sign a contract exclusively to them, that would prevent you from taking any other work. So, basically, your acting career would be over, you would be known as Mr K forever. My agent at that time was of course putting pressure on me to sign, not surprising, seeing as she would be taking fifteen per cent of a rather large fee. So, with added encouragement from home, I accepted.

The plot for the series was a family of four, dad, mum, a son, plus his wife. Mum and dad would have retired and were now running a bed and breakfast hotel in the country. That way, we would be able to have many different visitors in the hotel, which in turn would showcase all Kellogg's brands. If all this had gone to plan, we would have made three TV commercials a year In South Africa, Radio ads, Magazine ads, plus, the opening of Supermarkets, and our images on all Kellogg's products. All this at an agreed fee, of a quarter of a million pounds a year. In the late eighties, a lot of money then. A lot of money now.

The first two we would film, would be shot in Cape Town, South Africa (another good reason for taking the job). A cottage was built in the South African countryside, that resembled Surrey. That would stay, and we would go back every January to make two more. The reason being, Kellogg's is called, "The Sunshine Breakfast" and the light they wanted, could not be beaten in South Africa. What a beautiful country South Africa is.

John Lyons

I flew out with the woman who played my wife, the boy who was my son, plus his wife. The added player was Fred Dibnah, the steeplejack, (he would be the first guest in the series). What a lovely fellow he was. I got on very well with dear Fred, we did giggle a lot, maybe too much for the film's director. Once filming was over, myself, Fred, and the woman who played my wife, decided to hire a car, and take the opportunity to explore the wine estates of the south, and picnic on Table Mountain. Wonderful.

We did at one point have a long lunch at the two Oceans Restaurant on the very tip of South Africa, so called because it overlooked the Atlantic Ocean one side, and the Indian on the other. It was a long lunch, with quite a bit of wonderful South African wine consumed. I then made the mistake of asking Fred about the women in his life. A big mistake. Within four minutes, he was in floods of tears, brought on by some bad memories, and a lot of wine.

It did, after a while become a little embarrassing, what with Fred getting louder and louder, and the other diners looking at me as though it was my fault. What a great character. I did keep in touch with Fred once back in England and was very sad when I read of his passing. The rest of the year, we made only one more commercial, but this time in Surrey itself, seeing that it was the height of our summer, plus a photo shoot for Woman's Own, and that was that. Which brought me up to the end of my first twelve-month contract.

One day, before that contract expired, the advertising agency had conducted a survey to judge whether the campaign was having any effect on the public. It was most certainly not. Which meant, the day before the new contract would have come into force, they pulled the plug. Although this job was a very lucrative one, I strangely was relieved. The decision had been taken out of my hands, and I could carry on with work that was for me far more satisfying.

Chapter Fourteen:
Not All Work

Away from work, I got a call from a lovely Irishman by the name of Kevin O'Shea. Kevin had been running a showbiz football team for quite a while. Would I, and he would very much like me to, play this coming Sunday down in Welling in Kent. This for me, was the beginning of twenty-four years, playing Sunday football for the Top Ten Eleven, all over the country. I of course could not turn out every week, which was the same for all celebs, work permitting.

Over the years, some very big names would turn out on a Sunday. Rod Stewart for one. (Apart from his singing, Rod was a very good footballer) Tommy Steele, Bill Oddie, David Hamilton, (what a flying winger he was) Lonnie Donegan and many more. All very big names at the time. And still are. One of my great pleasures, was when we played alongside ex-professional players. Bobby Moore, Terry Venables, George Cohen and ex- England and Spurs Centre Forward, Bobby Smith. We would travel all over the country, most of the time by coach, or, if it were further afield like Jersey, Scotland or Wales, we would fly.

Many years before, when I was about fourteen, my friend Barry and I were in Soho waiting outside the Stage Door of the London Hippodrome, waiting for Lonnie Donegan who was topping the bill, to come out, in the hope of getting his autograph. Eventually he did. "Mr Donegan can I have your autograph please."

Without looking at me, He walked straight past, and out
of the corner of his mouth said, " PISS OFF." Now twenty-four years later, I'm playing football alongside him
somewhere in London. My wife is with me at the time,
and Lonnie had his wife as well. The four of us got on so
well, he invited us back to his lovely house in Chiswick for
drinks.

While he showed me around the house, with all the gold
records on the wall, I told him that story. "I didn't say that
did I?"

"Oh yes you did," says I.

"I'll find some paper, and give it to you now."

"PISS OFF" says I, with great satisfaction after all those
years. He was such a nice man, and a great entertainer. If
you don't know his work, look it up on YouTube.

Lonnie had a new and great sound, which many groups
took inspiration from. I saw his son in concert recently,
carrying on where his old man left off, very good, but a
hard act to follow. During those years of playing for the
Top Ten Eleven, I met, and became lifelong friends with the
likes of "Dave Dee" Remember? (Dave Dee, Dozy, Beaky
Mick and Titch) Junior Campbell, founder of the pop group
"Marmalade", pop stars, Jess Conrad and Troy Dante, and
top stunt man Rocky Taylor.

At one time, four of us got together and invested in a
greyhound, based at Wimbledon dog track. He, the dog,
was called "Devastated Chap" after Mr Troy Dante. I wish
I could remember why; it was a long time ago. I'm not
a gambler, but we did have some wonderful nights there
along with our families. Plus, that dog came up trumps
quite a few times.

Not Just George

At one point around this time, I left for a tour of Scotland with the Traverse Theatre Company based in Edinburgh. We were doing a production of Harold Pinter's "The Caretaker", in which I played the part of Mick. "The Caretaker" only has three characters in the cast, so when we finished our run at the Traverse, the company gave the three of us a car, to travel to and from the other venues the length and breadth of Scotland. This was in the winter months, and although it was very cold, I did find Scotland and the Scottish Highlands a most beautiful country. I have been back once or twice since then.

There was a time when Dave Dee, was the head of a company that took out tours of Sixties Pop Groups. Some of these groups were very big in the sixties, and some still are, The Tremeloes, Marty Wilde, The Searchers to name but three. These tours became very popular and travelled all over. From Ireland to the Canary Islands, and then, all over England. My part was to act as compere for the shows. I couldn't do every date, but quite a few. What fun we had. A little too much drink was consumed along the way as you can imagine with pop groups, but great fun.

Chapter Fifteen:
The High Seas

One Monday morning I found myself on a train with a director heading for Dartmouth in Devon, to film my very first episode of "The Onedin Line". I had been cast the previous week to play one of the regular crew members.

The next morning, I met up with the other cast members and we set off in two boats, the main one a large mast sailing ship, and the smaller, a supply boat carrying both cameras and crew. The day started off fine, sunny, and warm. As the two boats sailed further and further out to sea, it began to blow up quite a bit. My storyline in the first episode was to volunteer to go down into the hold where a fire had broken out and was threatening to destroy the ship. Thus, making me a hero.

Off we go. I volunteer to the Captain and make my way down through the smoke into the heart of the fire. Like all heroes I manage single handed to put the fire out and save the ship. The next shot is me, being pulled up unconscious from the hold, laid on the deck, where a bucket of sea water is then thrown over me and I regain consciousness. Before we could complete the next setup of me coming round, I had to have a quick word with the director and the producer. We had now been out at sea for at least two hours and severe seasickness had got a hold of me. There was still another full day's filming to go, and another five days that week.

I told both of them "I don't think I can go on any longer," I begged them to please "PLEASE, GET ME OFF THIS SHIP."

After a long discussion with the writer, they agreed, and sent for a small boat to come out and take this big butch actor back to the safety of land. It took an hour to complete this, but I was at last back in my hotel room, in bed, watching the ceiling of my room go round and round. The way the writer and director got around this incident was this – when I was laid out on the deck and the bucket of water was thrown over my face, there was a slow fade out, on me.

Cutting now to a scene that had never before been seen. James Onedin, the owner, is seen, comforting my wife who was holding two crying children and telling her "What a brave man your husband was, and how deeply sorry they all were."

So, there we are. They killed me off. I think I must be the only actor in the whole of Equity, to beg to be let go after only my first scene in a top BBC series. What a hero?

One funny moment occurred just after lunch. (There were not many laughs that day) to get out of the way of the cameras when you yourself were not filming, you were asked to go and sit downstairs. Sitting downstairs was not as easy as all that. The only place to sit was on one of the beams that ran across the ship, with your feet dangling in the smelly bilge on the bottom.

There I sat, feeling dreadful, alongside the writer of that week's episode, also in a very bad way. We both must have sat there for at least thirty minutes without speaking, or even looking at one another, wishing we were elsewhere. Eventually, he slowly turned to me and said, "This is the last time I go on a Clarkson cruise".

I think I laughed at the time, or maybe just offered a weak smile. But it was a very funny line at that moment.

Family: In the middle:
grandmother, left to
right: Mum, sister Kit,
cousin Eileen, brother
Joe. (Author's collection)

Child photo of me at
five: Butter wouldn't
melt in his mouth
(Author's collection)

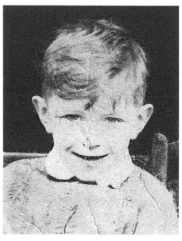

Mum and dad on a
rare holiday. (Author's
collection)

Wedding: Ann and I just married. 1965. (Author's collection)

My very first job. With Anthony Booth. 1964. (Author's collection)

Football. Top Ten Eleven: Rod Stewart (far right) Tommy Steele (far left) Middle: Bill Oddie, David Hamilton (Author's collection.)

Max Miller: Playing Max Miller, along with other parts in the West End for two years in the 70's. (Author's collection)

Paul Daniels and Debbie McGee, myself, Ann. Working the ships. (Author's collection.)

On the Buses: Myself and Bob Grant (Author's collection)

Britannic Money: Charles Darwin & me as Edward Elgar in TV advert (Author's collection)

Steve McQueen: Steve's younger brother? (Author's collection)

Sweeney Episode: Mid-seventies. (Author's collection)

Spooner's Patch - 4 people in shot. Patricia Hayes, William. G Stewart, getting too familiar with some bird (me). (Author's collection)

"Well, Nobody's Perfect" Spooner's Patch. Standing by car in drag – 'Not just George!'. (Most definitely Author's collection)

Spooner's Patch. Me and Patricia Hayes: (Author's collection)

Spooner's Patch. Left to right: Ronnie Fraser, Johnny Speight, myself, Ray Galton (pre Wimbledon boozy lunch) (Author's collection)

John Virgo: Snooker champion and my panto champion. (Author's collection)

Jim Davidson (The General"). One of seven pantos with Jim. (Author's collection)

Keith Barron. A lovely
man. (Author's collection)

Taken by Laura Ann Witt
(My daughter during
filming of "A TOUCH OF
FROST." (Author's own
collection)

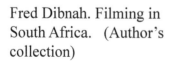

Fred Dibnah. Filming in
South Africa. (Author's
collection)

Brian Murphy.
One of many
nights at Joe
Allen's Restau-
rant. (Author's
collection)

Brian Conley. Working
P & O cruise ships.
(Author's collection)

The Mouse-
trap. My
first of three
differ-
ent casts.
(Author's
collection)

Barbara Windsor. A dear woman I have known since the sixties. (Author's collection)

Barbados. Ann and I on tour with P & O. (Author's collection)

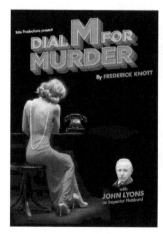

Dial M for Murder. Great production at the Playhouse Nottingham (by courtesy Karen Henson)

Ann and my daughter Laura, appearing as extras in the last episodes of "A TOUCH OF FROST" (Author's collection)

Amanda Barrie and me – panto (by courtesy Paul Holman Associates)

Golfing Photo. John H Stracey (boxing champion), myself, Jess Conrad (pop star) , Peter Shilton (England goalkeeper). (Author's collection)

Frost, Mullet and Toolan (Author's collection)

Chapter Sixteen:
Lionel Bart And Joan

Back in London Joan Littlewood had not forgotten me and I'm glad to say we were still friends. This is where the song writer Lionel Bart enters my life. I had already been in a production of "Fings Ain't What They Used To Be," which had been written by him along with Frank Norman, and had been a very big West End hit.

Now they were hoping to follow it up with a new musical called "Costa-Packet". This was to be set in Spain full of Brits on a two-week package holiday. We rehearsed this show for eight long weeks, trying to make something out of it. We then ran for another four weeks at Stratford. But, to no avail. It sank very quickly.

At this point Lionel had been working on a new production based on the legend of Robin Hood. This was going to be directed by Joan Littlewood and was going to be her very first commercial venture. The musical was to be called "Twang". The first day's rehearsal and read through took place at Lionel's beautiful house just off the Fulham Road, with a very large pink flamingo statue on the roof. How showbiz can you get? There that day were what looked like half of Equity – Ronnie Corbett, Bernard Bresslaw, Alfie Bass, Bob Grant etc. Alongside James Booth who would play Robin and Barbara Windsor who would play the part of Maid Marian.

Not Just George

By the end of the first week's rehearsal, there were by now, so many of us in the show, Jimmy Booth, playing the lead (Robin) had only about ten lines in the first act. The beginning of the next week, Joan took me aside and told me she would be leaving this project, it wasn't her thing. She said Gerry (her Manager) wanted to take out another tour of "Oh! What a Lovely War" and wanted me to go with it.

"Joan" I said, "I've just signed the contract for this show."

"Don't worry about that, I'll get you out of it, plus your rehearsal money," and she did.

So, I left and went out again around the country with a new company headed by Brian Murphy, and Joan went off to France where she was always very happy. "Twang" itself carried on, although a few names fell by the wayside. Jimmy Booth and Barbara however, stayed with it. It opened in Manchester to very bad reviews.

An American Show Doctor, Bert Shevlove, was brought over in the hope of pulling it together. After more rehearsals and quite a few changes and cuts, it finally moved into the Shaftesbury Theatre in London. If anything, the reviews were not much better, and I'm sorry to say it did not have a very long run. A great disappointment for Lionel in particular, and all those who stayed with it. Within the business the title "Twang" became known as THUD. A great shame.

Off I go once more with a new production and cast for "Oh! What a Lovely War." We reached the Theatre Royal Brighton one wintery Monday. By the matinee on Tuesday, I was feeling very rough. At the interval I could hardly stand. Our company manager told me to go to the chemist, which I did, load up with all kinds of medicines, and go back to the flat I was staying in that week with Brian and Larry Dann. That is of course what I did. While other members of the cast took over all my parts for the rest of the week.

That's where I stayed. In bed with a very severe case of the flu. I could hardly move out of my bed, and with no mobile phones at that time, I couldn't even phone my wife. Brian and Larry at this point, were afraid to come anywhere near me, just in case. At one point the bedroom door opened ajar, a hand came around the door with two slices of toast on a plate and was quickly shut again before I could even cry for HELP.

By the Friday it was obvious I was not going to return that week or the next, so our company manager got in touch with my wife and she in turn got our good friend Nobby, to drive down from London to Brighton in my car, pick me up, and return me home. I missed at least fourteen performances, which is only the second time in my life I have been off. That tour lasted for another six months.

My agent by now, is encouraging me to stop touring for a while, and concentrate on getting more TV work. She was true to her word. Over the next four years, I appeared in three different "Plays for Today" for the BBC. At that time, they were the mainstay of the BBC's drama output. "Spend, Spend, Spend", "A story to Frighten the Children" and "Moss".

This in particular was a very good one for me, playing the son of Warren Mitchell. A very sad story, which called for a lot of emotion from all characters (not exactly "On the Buses"). In the middle of rehearsing this particular play, we were situated on the sixth floor of the BBC rehearsal rooms, in Acton, West London. A large building, with two big rehearsal rooms on each floor, plus toilet facilities between each one. This was known as the "Acton Hilton" owing to its wonderful roof restaurant.

During one of our coffee breaks, I take the opportunity of a quick visit to the toilet. I'm standing there, at the urinal on my own, minding my own business, when the door opens behind me, and in walks the famous American actor, ZERO MOSTEL. He is over in this country rehearsing an opera, for which he will be the narrator. Back home in America, this man had been a very big Broadway star for many years. He having been the very first "Tevye" in "Fiddler on the Roof" the lead in "A Funny Thing Happened On The Way to The Forum" both on stage and film. And of course. the lead, alongside Gene Wilder, in Mel Brooks " THE PRODUCER'S " playing Max Bialystock. A worldwide hit.

Here he is now, this man, standing about six foot three, about twenty stone, maybe getting on in years, and needing the help of a walking stick. Zero slowly makes his way across the room and steps up the small step to reach the urinal next to me. He places his stick in front of him, and unzips. As he starts to pee, he gives me a look and says "Oh, thank God, it still works". We both laugh. With that, his foot slips off the step, and he starts to go backwards across the room, with his tiny member still out, still peeing down his trousers. Finally, he hits the far wall, crash, and slowly slips down into a sitting position. I pull myself together and run over to assist in any way I can. This man is far too big and heavy for me to lift, So, I say to him, "Don't move I'll get help."

I go next door to the room in which he is rehearsing and inform his floor manager of the problem. With that we both go back into the toilet, and there is Mr Mostel still in the sitting position, but now, thank God he has stopped peeing. We pick him up between us and sit him on a chair that the Floor Manager has brought with him and gives him the glass of water that I'm carrying. After a while, when we think he's recovered his composure, and the floor manager says a thank you to me, we all go back into our rehearsal rooms.

John Lyons

When I got home that night, I of course couldn't wait to tell my wife. The next morning when I arrive back in Acton, our floor manager hands me a letter. I open it and read: "Would you please give my thanks and love to the young man who helped me out in the men's toilet yesterday afternoon. I won't forget him." Signed Z.

When I get home Ann says "Where's that letter?"

I look in my bag. "Oh! I must have left it in the rehearsal room." I quickly call back, but no answer. All gone home. Next morning when I get in early to search – gone! The cleaners have been in early and it's now part of the building's rubbish. What a shame. That could have been a collector's item. I could at least have left it to the Theatre Museum.

Up popped London Weekend Television once more, with an offer of seven episodes of a new comedy called "Both Ends Meet". This was starring Dora Bryan and Wendy Richard. I of course did them with pleasure, but nothing much happened with the project, and like so many others before, it just disappeared. As I mentioned earlier, meeting and working for casting agents in commercials and small student films, with a bit of luck, would pay off in the years ahead, as they 'the agents' moved on to bigger things.

One such became a very important person in my life. Her name, Marilyn Johnson. Yes, she had started off small, but now, was one of the top casting agents in the country. She went on to cast productions of Cracker, Minder, Boon and so on. Marilyn called my agent one day and asked if I would go along to Euston Films, to read for an episode of "The Sweeney." The Sweeney in the 1970s, was a very big hit at the time, and still stands up very well today starring John Thaw and Dennis Waterman.

All episodes were filmed on location in and around London over a two-week period. It was a very tight schedule, which meant that both John and Dennis could be working on two episodes at the same time. Dennis Waterman I had known for quite a few years through playing football together, and John Thaw I had worked with on his very first leading role on television "Redcap". This was set around a military police unit. The Sweeney episode I featured in was titled "Bad Apple". It's worth looking at now not only for the story and the action, but also the dialogue, fashion, and hairstyles of the day.

Marilyn cast me again two years later in the second Sweeney film, in which we spent a week in Malta, and five weeks in West London robbing banks. Great fun being a kid. One of the lovely things I remember about John Thaw was that he never forgot my name.

When you think, that over the years starring in so many TV series, he must have met and worked with hundreds of actors, and sometimes there would be gaps of five or six years between our meeting, but he never forgot. He also remembered the names of my characters in those past productions. I don't know if he did this with other actors, but it was very special for me. John was such a very good actor, very professional and so kind to fellow artists. After the "Sweeney" he went on to other big hits like 'Kavanagh QC' and 'Morse' – which became a hit all over the world.

While I think of actors being not only professional and kind to other artists, I must tell you about an incident which happened on an episode of the original 'Upstairs Downstairs.' My first day on this episode was for the read through. This was held at the Duke of York's Barracks in Chelsea. I had trouble finding a parking space that day, so consequently, was late arriving at the given time of ten o'clock.

The Duke of York's Barracks is an enormous building as

you can imagine. with two great big doors guarding its entrance. Once I got myself through them, I found I was standing in a very large, what looked like a ballroom, with all of the cast, director, producer and the rest of their team sitting around a large oval table on the far side of this large ballroom. Now, I have to make my way across it to join them, with all eyes focused on me in dead silence. I could hear my own footsteps.

Now this is where Mr Gordon Jackson came to my rescue. Being the professional that he was, he must have quickly looked down at the cast list, stood up, and in a loud voice said "John! How lovely to see you again, join us dear boy." He then met me halfway, shook my hand, and introduced me to the rest of the cast. I had never met him before in my life.

Obviously, he had seen the embarrassing position I was in, and may have been in a similar position himself over the years. A new cast member coming into a long successful series, in which everyone else knew each other. Not easy. Gordon Jackson had been in the business for many years, with a very impressive record of work behind him with many British and Hollywood films to his credit. In this particular vehicle (Upstairs, Downstairs) he played the Butler 'Hudson', and went on to another hit series a few years later, 'The Professionals' in which he played 'Cowley' Head of C15. As I say, what a pro.

One television programme I have not mentioned, simply because I do not know into what category it fits. Comedy or drama? You choose. "Crossroads" The original one with Noele Gordon. Crossroads was an ATV production filmed at their small studio in Birmingham. In one week, they would film four half hour episodes.

Monday would start with the read through, then rehearse Tuesday, Wednesday and Thursday morning. Film the first episode on Thursday afternoon and second episode on Friday along with episodes three and four. What a tight schedule. Was it any wonder that in that small studio, you would sometimes see the set shake when an actor came through a door? Or, on quite a few occasions, an actor would stumble over his lines with a look of bewilderment on his face. They would never stop running unless something really bad had happened.

You were encouraged to carry on regardless. I just went in for those four episodes playing a jewel thief. Then I disappeared for good. Thank heavens. On that schedule, if I had been in it for six months, I would have had a nervous breakdown. Being in many TV Sitcoms was never easy. Think of this. You would start on Monday morning with a read through, then rehearse in the afternoon. Again Tuesday, producers run on Wednesday, camera rehearsal Thursday, two run-throughs on Friday, then the recording Friday night, IN FRONT OF A LIVE AUDIENCE. That was never easy. This would be the one and only time you would have an audience. So, you had no idea if there would be a laugh on certain lines, or silence. Plus, you were working to two mediums, TV and Theatre.

About twenty years ago, I played a Court Judge, in a daytime soap, "Family Affairs" for Channel Five. I had one day's filming in a real Court, but that day, they got enough filming out of me, that could be used in five different episodes. That could be in the Guinness Book of Records. Five episodes in one day. A long day. The script I got, had numbers for every line. The director would say "John, lines ten to twenty-one" and that's how it went on. That's what's known as "acting by numbers."

Chapter Seventeen:
Jobs I Didn't Get

Back in the early 1960s whilst still at drama school, Philip Headley who helped me in many ways, left after our second year. Apart from being a very fine actor, Philip went on to be an even better director. At one time he directed at the Theatre Royal Lincoln, and then for many years ran the Theatre Royal Stratford E15 after Joan Littlewood had left. While he was there, I worked for him on at least three occasions, as well as a spell for him in Lincoln, in a production of "Marie Lloyd" in which the actress, Jean Boht gave a great performance.

Sometime in the mid-70s, Philip got together a new musical written by Ken Lee, showing how Britain got through the Second World War, this show was comprised of songs of the time, and scenes all based around the war effort at home. The musical started out in Watford, but very quickly transferred into the West End, finding itself ensconced at the Ambassadors Theatre. After its first year's run, some of the original cast decided to move on to other pastures. At this point, Philip called and asked if I could come along and see the show on Monday night, with a view of taking over certain characters within it.

Ann and I watched that night's performance, and by the interval I was sold. This was right up my street. Each actor and actress were playing six or seven different roles. There were songs, dances, and comedy. I said yes the very next morning. This new cast had only two weeks rehearsal before opening, and we stayed together very happily for the next eighteen months.

At one point in the middle of this show, I came on playing Winston Churchill, giving one of his wartime speeches "We shall never surrender". As I got off, a dresser very quickly took off my very large coat and Homburg hat, folded down my brightly covered trouser legs, passed me my Trilby and I was straight back on again to do five minutes patter as the very popular comedian of the time," Max Miller." That's the way the show progressed. Great fun.

I did enjoy those eighteen months. Although my father never lived long enough to see me do anything on the stage, my sister, brother and dear mum did. She loved it. It brought back great memories for her. some sad, some happy. Although she would never say it to me, I knew she was proud. The show was "Happy as a Sandbag" Now I'm not a gambler, I've always thought that being an actor was a big enough gamble – it's a very strange way to earn a living if you think about it. In our union, Equity, there are about 48,000 members, Men, women, boys and girls of all ages, colour, and size, and probably another four thousand who are not members, because nowadays you do not have to be a member of the Union to get work.

Out of all those members, at any time, there would be at least 80% out of work, and it seems to be getting worse – what with all the reality shows we now have on our screens. It seems to me that work is becoming much harder to find. Especially for the younger actor. It helps greatly if you have a thick skin. Throughout your career you will be turned down, rejected for many jobs, not because you can't do them, but for many other reasons.

You don't match your fellow actor, you're too young, too old, the wrong accent etc. Many reasons. If you take all this rejection personally, you will not last. In all the years I've

John Lyons

been in this daft business, there have been quite a few jobs I've been up for and didn't get. At the Mermaid Theatre in the City of London, every year they put on a big production of "Treasure Island." Most of the time starring Spike Milligan. I went and auditioned one year for Bernard Miles, who at that time ran the theatre, and his then director.

The next day, they called my agent and said "Thank John for coming, he did very well. Unfortunately, we can't use him because he's too tall for the set." I didn't get the job. (I could have bent my knees.)

I had an audition for a D.H. Lawrence Play at the Royal Court Theatre in London. Sitting in his office with the director, about to do a reading, he says, "John, this accent is thirteen miles outside Nottingham."

I said "David, I can do twelve and a half, but I'm not sure about thirteen."

He didn't laugh. I DIDN'T GET THE JOB. My own fault, trying to be too clever. Miriam Brickman in the 1960s and 70s was a topflight casting agent. Major films including Bond, Straw Dogs etc. She had asked me to come along for an audition at her very small flat in Half Moon Street Mayfair. I turn up on time, I always try to be early, gives you time to settle yourself. Miriam opens her door, with a strange, embarrassed look on her face. All she could say to me was "Hello John, thank you for coming."

Standing almost on her shoulder was a very attractive American woman. We go on into her small living room, and placed in the middle, facing each other, are two ordinary kitchen chairs. I'm shown to the one facing back to the door. The young woman sits opposite me. She is going to conduct the interview. Off we go, with the usual questions – what have you been doing recently? Have you had any filming experience? And so on.

Halfway through, I looked beyond her, and in the corner, behind the door is a man sitting in the corner dressed in what looks like a large old army coat, with a hat pulled down over his eyes. He is hunched over a small desk writing. He never seemed to look up, but obviously he was listening. Suddenly, I look at the young American woman interviewing me, and it registers. It's Diane Keaton. I look back at the man hunched in the corner, it's Woody Allen.

Of course, silly me! At the time, these two were an item. Mr Allen never looked at me once, never said anything, just carried on writing. At the end of the interview, after Ms Keaton thanked me for coming, we all stood, and I couldn't help myself but say to the mystery man in the corner, very sarcastically "Nice to meet you Mr Allen. We must do this again sometime." Silly of me.

Now I understood why Miriam Brickman looked so very embarrassed. Mr Allen had behaved this way in every interview that day. Quite a few actors were upset by the way he treated people and told him so. I DIDN'T GET THE JOB. Nor did many British actors. The film was called "Love and Death." If you watch it, there is only one British actor in it - Aubrey Morris. All the rest either didn't get it or turned it down.

Another film role I didn't get was the time I was summoned to the Atheneum Hotel in Piccadilly, London, to meet a director by the name of Fraser Hefton. My appointment is for 10:30, I arrive at ten. I've been told by my agent that my photos have been seen back in the States, and they are now seeing actors for a production of "Treasure Island" (I hope this time I'm not too tall!).

I announce myself at the hotel reception, and I'm asked to take a seat in the lobby, and the receptionist will inform them I'm here. Time passes. Finally, they must have got tired of waiting for the casting director to arrive and

call down to ask me to go on up to suite 606. Up I go.
Sixth floor. Suite 606. Right. I take a deep breath and
knock. The door opens and there stands a young man, with
glasses and a rather high American voice.

"Hi John, come on in." I walk with him down the corridor
into the vast living room. "John, meet my Dad."

Dad, sitting in a large armchair, gets to his feet, and with
a voice that makes the room shake says "Hi John, come
on in, sit over here". It's Charlton Heston. My agent has
made a mistake in the names. The young boy in glasses is
not Fraser Hefton, but Fraser Heston.

Mr Heston's son, Fraser will be directing the film, with his
father playing "Long John Silver." I am now transfixed on
this giant of a man, looking at him with my mouth open. He
is talking away, about what, I don't know.

My mind is racing. I answer back, but although words are
coming out of my mouth, in my mind I'm saying "My God,
it's Ben Hur, it's Moses! What's that great film he did with
Orson Wells? Yes," A Touch of Evil." All this whilst he is
still talking to me. He must have noticed I was in a state
of slight disarray because he got up from his armchair and
asked if I wanted a glass of water.

"Yes, please Sir." I called him Sir! He got up and made his
way over to a sideboard to pour two glasses.

My mind now says to me "My word, he's a bit dodgy on
his pins." After he has passed the water to me, he slowly sat
down.

Again, I can't stop talking to myself "Is that a wig? No, it
can't be". He settles himself and asks if I would like to read
one or two scenes.

"Yes please" I reply. Not knowing if I'm even up to it. My
new friend "Chuck" hands me two colour coded scripts,

which comprise the scenes I am there for. Off we go, reading together. I can hear him, but I can't hear myself, it all sounded gibberish to me. At the end, he put his script away, asked me to kindly leave mine on the side table, and thanked me very much for taking the time. Fraser, his son, showed me to the door and said the old words "We'll be in touch with your agent." I DIDN'T GET THE JOB.

It transpires that the casting agent, my old friend Marilyn Johnson, was stuck on the London Underground between Piccadilly Circus and Hyde Park Corner, due to a faulty train signal. This meant she was out of communication for an hour and a half. If she had joined me in the hotel reception and put me wise that I would be reading with Charlton Heston, I probably would have still been slightly nervous, but would have had time to pull myself together, and give a far better account of myself. Great shame. What a job. It comprised of one weeks filming at the Docks in Bristol, followed by six weeks in Jamaica, alongside Christian Bale and Oliver Reed. All this disappeared before me, owing to a faulty train signal. Again, that's show business.

One film I did get, was for the director Michael Winner. I found myself seated in his wonderful big house in Kensington, opposite who I believed to be either his assistant, or his secretary. Mr Winner himself was not present. If he had been watching this interview via closed circuit TV, I don't know. There were certainly many cameras guarding his estate. Before I left the house, I was informed the part was mine. The part consisted of only one, but a fairly long scene, playing the security officer on the Orient Express. Finally, I got my call to be at a small studio in West London, and I'm shown to my own trailer.

There, costume and full make-up are waiting for me. As I look down at the call sheet for this scene, I see the two actors I am sharing this scene with are two unknowns -

John Lyons

Michael Caine and Roger Moore! My word. In full costume, make up and wig I sit in my trailer all day, and the next. The first assistant at the end of the first day, apologises for keeping me waiting, and informs me they are running late. This goes on for five further days.

By the end of the fifth day, I'm now not worried at all about playing a scene with two Hollywood superstars, even if I do have all the dialogue, and I'm being directed by a man, Michael Winner, who didn't have a very good reputation when it comes to working with actors. Sitting on my own, in full costume, make up and wig, unable to venture out, it became worse than sitting outside the Dentist's room waiting for a root canal procedure.

Eventually I get my call. "We're ready for you now Mr Lyons." I make my way to the set and enter. Mr Winner just looks at me, and then turns to whisper something to his assistant. Straight away, both Hollywood stars approach. "Hello son, what's your name?"

"John," I reply.

"Hello John, I'm Michael" (as if I don't know). "And this is Roger."

In that wonderful deep voice that we've all heard for many years, "Hello dear boy, welcome aboard."

I knew I was in safe hands with these two. Both had been around the block many times and knew how to treat an actor coming on to the set for the first time, amongst everyone else who had been together for weeks. My mind went back to dear Gordon Jackson. It makes sense. You will get better work out of the person if he is relaxed and comfortable, then if he is nervous and in awe of it all.

The only time Mr Winner ever said anything to me, was when he gave me my directions, and after I performed, which was a tricky piece of business, which involved a fake spear going through my head. In between the first and second take, he patted me on the back and said quietly "You're working well Sir." He hadn't even bothered to learn my name.

One lovely moment happened in a lunch break. I'm back in the make up trailer having my make up retouched. When in walks Mr Roger Moore holding a paper bag full of Mars Bars and Marathons, which he then passes out to all the make-up ladies. He then looks at me and says, "I won't offer you one John; you've still got dialogue to do." What a wonderful pro. Plus, HE had LEARNT my name. The film was called "Bullseye." I think it played one week at the Odeon Marble Arch, then went straight to video.

My last little venture with Hollywood came from the management team of (wait for it…!) Steve McQueen. Somehow, they had seen photographs of me and asked my agent if they could have some more, plus a CV of my work. The reason being, they were in the process of looking for a young actor to play the part of Steve McQueen's younger brother in an upcoming film and thought I might fit the bill.

Well, of course, between my agent and myself, we got together a package and sent it off. Nothing happened. Still waiting. I thought it might be a daft prank, but no. My agent made enquiries over there, and it was on the level. It just got shelved as most of them do. While thinking about American films. I have been asked, on a few occasions, what was it like working on "The Blues Brothers?"

I've no idea, I wasn't in it. If you were to look up my name on IMDB, you will see I'm credited with being in that very clever film, along with "Action Jackson" and in this country, "Shameless." The only reason I can think of is, that an actor in America has the same name as me. I seem to get his credits, and he must get mine. Poor devil.

John Lyons

He must get asked all the time, "What was it like working in "On the Buses" and "George and Mildred?" As for "Shameless" I have been told, they had an extra working on one episode, with the same name as mine. He, at the last minute was given a couple of lines to say. Which meant he was given a credit. No one had checked this out with our union Equity. Which states that no two actors can have the same names. Makes sense, can you imagine the problems that could cause?

A question most actors get asked is, "What do you prefer, TV or Theatre?" It's a good question. I always answer, and I'm sure most of us do, "Theatre every time." Television and film are, most of the time, very quick, but pay well. Theatre, on the other hand, does not pay half as well. (Unless you're lucky enough to be in the West End.) But theatre is where you will get the most satisfaction.

When working on TV or film, you get a very limited time to rehearse, and hardly ever the chance to do a scene more than two or three times (they of course want you to get it right on the first take). Then, that's gone for good. Also, the schedule would have been worked out in the pre-production planning, meaning that almost all scenes will not be in story order.

So, you could start the first day playing a scene, that is in fact, the last scene in the play. Confusing? But true. Once or twice, I have arrived on set, to be introduced to the actress who will play my wife. Difficult. Especially if the husband and wife in the storyline have been married for say, thirty years. A couple who have been married for that length of time would have a different attitude towards each other, and probably display a different body language. That attitude has to be worked out pretty quick.

Back on stage, the minimum time you normally get to rehearse, is two weeks. If you're very lucky, it can stretch to three. This way, you have the luxury of, working on the script, trying out different ways of playing it, with the help of the director, and getting to know your fellow actors. Once that play opens, you will play that same part, eight times a week. Maybe, as I have been lucky to have done, a run of one, or two years. I always found, after the first month, I would look back, and see how different I was playing it now, as opposed to when we started that first week. That's a good thing.

A lot of people seem to be interested in how actors learn all those lines. Well, it can be a very boring process, but one that I have come to enjoy. For a stage play, you do have a longer timeframe. I always ask the management if I can, to let me have the script as early as possible. They can't always oblige, but it is very helpful if they do.

For me, I like to learn those lines, forwards, backwards, sideways, in other words, until they become second nature. It does become a daily grind of going over and over that script page by page, until you get to the stage where you need another person to feed you the cues. That's where my dear wife makes an entrance. And very good she is. Not only picking me up when I go wrong, but also making the odd suggestion (which I ignore).

The only time when I myself feel safe and confident that I can go off the book, is when I can walk around the large park in front of our house, and go through the whole part in my head, without the aid of the script. The problem there is, I do forget myself sometimes, and start mouthing the words while walking. On the few occasions, I have noticed couples passing, and one would say to the other, "Look at that poor old sod, he's lost it". I'm only really satisfied when I can say to myself, "John, you know this part backwards, now just forget it, and listen to the other actor."

Easy to say, but hard to do. This way (with a bit of luck) the words should come out of your mouth in a naturalistic way. Another option is, if you are really up against it, and those words have to be committed to memory quickly, try writing them down on notepaper, as if you're writing home. By the physical effort of watching those words you're writing come out of that pen onto that paper, you will be amazed how you will be able to see that letter that you have just written in your mind's eye. I have used this little trick myself a few times on TV, or when having to make a speech at the last minute. The problem with this method is it doesn't last long in the old brain box. The next day, it's gone.

Chapter Eighteen: A Second String to My Bow

I often think to myself, this really is a strange profession to be involved in, a very insecure way to make a living. Whatever job you are working on, when it comes to its end, most of the time you've no idea where the next one will come from. You could be out of work for one week, or six. Strange, but in some perverse way, I quite like that feeling. The feeling of not knowing what your next job might be, who it could be with, or where. Strange. But I guess, after all these years, I've got used to it.

Back in the sixties whilst still a student at drama school and working nights at Stratford East, I became involved in a production called "What a crazy world". This was a new musical written by Alan Klein. He had written some very clever, catchy songs, with a fun plot to go with them. My function on this was, up top in the flies, letting down, and taking up sections of the set when required.

In between it gave me time to look down onto the stage, to watch and learn. I do remember the actor Harry H. Corbett (Steptoe and Son) being part of it. And I'm sure I'm right, that it was one of the very first professional appearances of a young Ray Winstone, but I wouldn't swear to that. Now, in the mid-seventies, Ken Hill (writer/director/actor)) was running the Theatre along with Larry Dann. They decided to resurrect "What a crazy world" which Larry would direct.

He asked me if I would like to be part of this fun show, which I did with great pleasure, for a five week run. A few years later it was made into a film starring pop stars Marty Wilde and Joe Brown. It's often shown today on TV, and well worth a watch. As the seventies were drawing to a close, Ann came home one afternoon from the doctors, with barely concealed excitement, and announced that she was pregnant. After fifteen years of marriage. That's what you could call, a long rehearsal.

So now, I've got to start growing up, and stop playing these silly games that we actors play. I have to start thinking ahead. Do I want to carry on going off on tours anymore for a year at a time, or off to Rep for maybe a six month stint? No, I do not. I want to be at home, watching my child grow up. When it was just Ann and I, if I went out on tour, she would come with me, and on occasions if need be, and we were in a town or City for a decent spell, she would find herself a job.

But now with a child on the way, things would have to be different. Now, I had to think about adding another string to my bow (which is what every actor should do anyway). I now go to see my agent and tell her, "I don't want to go on tours for a while, or long stints in Rep."

Of course, I still wanted to be put up for work, but they would have to be in or around London, so that I could be at home. What I was doing of course, was cutting my income in half. An idea came into my head one day, when I ran into an old friend who had a printing business that had been established many years before by his grandfather, "Victor Printing."

I thought about this idea for a week or so, and then approached him. Could I start a small printing business, to run alongside his? He in turn thought about it for a while and recognised it could be beneficial to both of us. And in turn would advise and help in any way he could. Which is exactly what I needed. I at this point, had not the slightest idea how a printing company worked, or even, what went into the process of print.

The first thing I did was to enroll in a printing course, not because I wanted to be a printer, or run a printing machine, but to find out the basics, and the process that had to be gone through, in order to produce the many sides of the printing process, I completed the course, and at the same time, bought a printing machine, which if need be, I could run myself. To my great surprise, in the first six months, I had acquired seven good customers, two or three quite big, the others slightly smaller.

This really is all I needed. Because, again to my surprise, acting jobs in or around London were still coming in. An episode of "Follyfoot". Remember that? Followed by "The Tomorrow People" for Thames TV. And three episodes of "U.F.O." for ATV. Ann was now approaching nine months, so to be close, I took a pantomime at Stratford East, "Dick Whittington" with my old friend Brian Murphy.

It was during this run, on the 16th of January 1980, she gave birth, after three days in labour, to a beautiful baby girl, Laura Ann. The reason I'm at Stratford in panto, is that Ann is in a hospital only two miles away. Which meant that before, and in between shows, I could visit. On a few occasions whist visiting, I did fall asleep in the armchair beside her bed. When the time came for me to leave, she would nudge me and say, "You'd better go, you'll miss the half."

What with doing two shows, running a printing business, and making visits to the hospital, I was knackered. A week later, I was able to take the both of them home, with the snow thick on the ground. At the time, we lived in a small, but nice flat, opposite the "Blind Beggar Pub" (Where Ronnie Kray shot George Cornell). Unfortunately, this flat was on the top floor, five flights up, with no lifts. This was not a great problem for Ann and I, but now with a small child, it would very quickly turn into one.

Around this time, my dear mum was beginning to show signs of becoming unwell. She was now living on her own, in a high rise block in Limehouse. This would be the first time she had lived alone. Never ever, having had a telephone at home, now she was on her own, I had one installed for her. I gave it a couple of days, and called. On her picking it up, I could just about hear a faint "Hello".

"Mum, it's me," again. "Hello, mum, it's me, turn the phone around," she was speaking into the wrong end. This was becoming more and more worrying, as she was beginning to forget important things, like leaving the gas on, leaving fires on all night, etc.

The problem, as the doctor explained to my brother and myself, was oxygen. Or the lack of it. In her case it was either not reaching the heart, or the brain. It turned out eventually to be her brain. Slowly over time, little brain cells were popping and dying, which was the cause of her forgetting many things.

While waiting for the doctors to find a place for her nearby, where she would be looked after twenty-four hours a day, Ann and I decided to have her stay with us for a while. Although we now had a child, my brother had three, and they also at that time, lived in a flat. So for him, it would be doubly difficult.

One very curious incident happened one evening. The only place we could find where my mother could sleep, was in my one-year-old daughter's bedroom. I had moved her cot into our room. As mum was getting herself ready for bed, I went in to check that everything was alright. Before I entered, I caught a glimpse of her through the crack of the open door. She was standing in the middle of the room, holding my daughter's full bottle of milk. As I watched, she undid the top, and slowly poured the contents onto the floor of the bedroom.

I gave it a few seconds, knocked on the open door and went in. "Oh dear" I say, "What happened mum?"

She looked at me and said, "Look what your Laura did."

She was putting the blame on a one-year-old child. Well, I helped her into bed, cleaned up the milk the best I could, and said goodnight. I thought about this strange happening a few months later, when by now she was in a care ward of a local hospital. On the occasions when my brother, sister and I would visit, she would often talk about things that happened in her childhood many years ago. A doctor had told me that this was something that often occurred, when the brain cells began to fade. My mind went back to that night in my daughter's small bedroom, with all the trappings of childhood spread around the room. Her mind must have gone back many years for just a moment. Fascinating.

One of the strangest subjects she spoke to me about was the black American Boxer "Jack Johnson." Now my mother had no interest in Boxing or sport whatsoever. But around the time she reached three or four, "Jack Johnson" became the first black Heavyweight Champion of the World. This was a big event all around the World.

For her, living in a house, with at that time, at least eight brothers, it would have been talked about constantly. She must have listened to all that, and took it all in. Now here we are, with me sitting at her bedside, and she is talking about an event that took place over seventy-five years earlier. After about five minutes, she stopped and came back to the present. Now, this was a sad thing for a son to witness, but at the same time, a fascinating thing to watch. How an event can stay locked in the back of the mind, and then find its way forward many years later.

She also reminded me of what I know to be my earliest memory. I was around about twelve months old, and still in my mother's arms, watching my dad climb onto the back of a lorry with other local men, going, I assume, to help with the bomb clearance. He would have been too old to have been in the Army. I often remember that incident myself. And now, here she is, years later confirming my own earliest memory. Incredible.

She passed away a few months later, but I'm so glad I had the time to sit and talk, although she didn't seem to understand much of what I was saying, and to be able to tell her certain things before she went. One of the things that has stayed with me, and something I regret to this day, happened on the last two visits I made to her in the care ward. There, she showed me bruising on both her arms and legs. She told me that "the staff were being very rough with me and were hurting me a lot."

When I looked at her arms and legs, they were indeed both bruised and slightly swollen. My thoughts were, and I explained it to her, that "No mum, they are not deliberately trying to hurt you, the bruising is the result of the injections they are giving you, plus, everyone's skin gets thinner as you get older. They are here to look after you mum, not harm you."

She shook her head slowly, looked at me and said quietly "All right son if you say so."

Now, this was forty years ago. Since then, we have all read, and seen closed circuit TV footage, which has indeed shown, that a lot of bad and harmful practices did go on in some, NOT ALL, care homes. But, at the time, I just couldn't believe these things went on. Now I know. My mum could well have been right. Which has always left me with the feeling of letting my dear mum down in her last days.

Chapter Nineteen: Luck or Fate?

Those five floors were now becoming a real problem, what with a child's pram, and everyday tasks like shopping. As you may have noticed, luck, or fate has seemed to have played a big part in my life. (So, see what you make of this.).

In the late seventies, Ann and I are in our local park one Sunday morning. The park itself is very big, and on a lovely summer's day it's full. It has tennis courts, a boating lake, even a running track. After spending a couple of pleasant hours, we start to make our way home. But, instead of walking back through the park, we take the slightly longer route, along the road that runs alongside the park.

A quarter of the way along, I stop outside one particular house. Ann is alongside me, but I'm transfixed on what I`m looking at. It must have seemed strange, and I guess very rude to the man who was sitting by his downstairs window, (which were two large glass doors) one open. He was sitting on a high back chair, with his legs crossed, sporting a full dark beard, and smoking a pipe. I even noticed he was wearing sandals. What struck me most, was that he looked so relaxed and content, sitting there looking out over this lovely park, puffing away on his pipe. I would imagine all this only took about fifty or so seconds before we moved on. But before we did, I said to Ann, "Wouldn't it be wonderful to live there?"

Fourteen years later, we moved into that very same house. What do you think, luck, or fate? I know where my money goes. Even today, we see couples doing exactly what we did many years ago. Standing on the pavement dreaming. Apparently, our good friend Nobby, (the one who drove down to Brighton to take me home) many years before, without me knowing anything about it, (Ann says she knew, but I didn't) had put our name down on the housing list.

He, for many years had lived in that same road. So now, here we are, a young couple with a two-year-old child, receiving a call saying "A house is about to become vacant, owing to the present family locating up to Leicester, would you both be interested?"

Would we be interested? Ann and I, with Laura in the back seat, were over there in twenty minutes flat. There we stood, outside the very house, where fourteen years previously I had said to Ann "Wouldn't it be wonderful to live there". I'm very glad to tell you that of course we did move in and have been very happy ever since (the place where that man sat, is now the place where I have my chair, but, without the pipe!)

Around this time, while working on a commercial for Ridley Scott, I met a man who came from Bethnal Green, by the nickname of Smuggler Bill. (Don't ask). William was much older than me, with a great Cockney sense of humour, and we became great friends. It was he who introduced me to the great pleasures of the Turkish baths.

This particular bath was a very famous one situated in Bethnal Green. Being down there was like being on the set of "Guys and Dolls". It seemed that everyone had a nickname. There was "Mosher Brown Bread", "Lenny the Dip", "Idol Izzy", apart from "Smuggler" (I think they had seen too many American films).

At one point I'm resting on the bed alongside Smugs, when a chap passed us saying hello to everyone. I say, "What's his name Bill?"

"That's Front Page Sam."

"How did he get the name Front Page Sam?"

"Because he knows all the news."

Of course, how silly of me. Another world. I'm sitting one day, outside the very hot steam room on my own, with only a towel around me, when I look to my right, and there's a middle-aged man, just arrived, also with just a towel around him, doing his stretching exercises up against the wall. I look again, and slowly it dawns on me. This man with his left leg half way up the wall is the world famous ballet dancer Rudolf Nureyev. My word.

I think I was the only one down there who knew who he was. Most of them probably thought he played for West Ham. When he had finished stretching his body, he began to walk towards me. I, in turn, slowly stood up, and made my way back into the steam room. Two minutes later, the door opens, and in steps "Rudy".

"Good Morning" he says.

"Morning."

He sits on the slab opposite me, "It's very hot, no?"

"Yes, yes very hot" I then notice in his hand he is holding a bar of soap.

He then hits me with the line, "Would you like me to give you a rub down with this soap?"

Oh dear. "No. No, I'm fine, Phew, my word, it is hot in here, I think I'll jump in the cold pool."

I think he should have jumped into the cold pool. I was out of there like a shot. I never told anyone else there that day, otherwise, the leading dancer at Covent Garden, may well have had three kneecaps. I saw him again two years later at a small theatre in London. He walked straight passed me. How quickly they forget.

I first met my old friend Smuggler Bill while filming a big commercial for Ridley Scott over in Spain. We all stayed at The Alhambra Palace Hotel overlooking the lovely city of Granada. There is a lovely piece of classical music called "Memories of the Alhambra". Look it up, have a listen, it's worthwhile. I have very fond memories of The Alhambra.

Over my years of using the Turkish baths, I made some very good friends, all for some reason much older than me. Most of them were Freemasons, and as time passed, three of them asked me to join them in their Lodge, Stoke Newington.

I thought about this for a while, and eventually I agreed, and spent the next twenty-five years a Freemason. Over those years, I of course started on the bottom rung of Freemasonry, Outer Guard, then Inner Guard, and so on. Until many years later, and a lot of hard work, I had worked my way through all the grades, ending up as Master of the Lodge.

This came with quite a responsibility, plus a lot of ritual to learn. As Master of the Lodge , you were expected to be on top of all proceedings and guide the Lodge through all the various stages of those meetings. I think, and I hope, I did a fairly good job. I do know that in my year of Office, we raised quite a lot of money for many different charities. At the end of your year in Office, you are given what is known as, a Ladies Night.

These nights take quite a lot of planning, but with the help of some very experienced members, mine was held at the Cafe Royal in Regent Street. What a wonderful evening that turned out to be. Ann, of course, being the wife of the Master of the Lodge, was the leading lady for the night. Ann's parents, along with my brother Joe, sister Kit and her husband were there that night, all enjoying a great evening. Dancing to a jazz band, eating, drinking, all compered by my old mate, DJ, David Hamilton.

It was only a few years later when I reluctantly had to leave my position in the Lodge. The reason being, that the Lodge itself met four times a year, from November to February. I at this time, had just started filming "A Touch of Frost" way up in Leeds. Plus, if not filming, I would be away somewhere else in the country involved in panto, which meant a clash of dates. So, after a few years of not being able to attend any meetings. I sadly had to resign.

Things at this time are going well. We are in our new house, our daughter has started school, and now, Ann has found herself a job at the local hospital. Plus, the acting jobs are ticking along nicely. Three episodes of "The Bill", the "Liver Birds" for the BBC, and the printing business is doing exactly as I planned it.

Six customers was all I wanted, or could cope with. A few big ones, like the Golf and Tennis Resort La Manga Club, Pine Cliffs Golf and Country Club and Four Seasons Resort. In between, a commodity broker in the City, and a solicitor's firm. At times, when I would be working as an actor, and needed to be seeing a client, it did become a bit difficult, having to be in two places at the same time. Somehow, I did it. Having my own business meant that I could, most of the time, be my own boss, and spend that time helping out, not only at home, but taking Laura to school, and collecting her in the afternoons.

Making time to be together as a family, has paid off greatly, we both, Ann and I, have a very close and wonderful relationship with our daughter Laura. Now, a lovely married woman. The printing business was not turning over a great deal of money, but it did make up for the money I was missing out on in the acting profession. What I did do, was to take out two pensions for later in life. Good move John. A great safety net in this profession. So, throughout the eighties all was progressing rather well.

Until we got to the beginning of the nineties. Then that terrible word "recession" raised its ugly head. Slowly but surely, all sorts of companies were beginning to experience cash flow problems. My big customers, who had their main offices in Central London, were looking for ways to cut costs, and were moving their printing output on site, over to Spain and Portugal.

Which meant, I lost them. Three other customers also went out of business very quickly, two of them owing me money. One for six thousand, and another for nine hundred pounds. There was no way I was going to get any of that back. I would be lucky to get ten pence in the pound. Plus, all TV companies began to tighten their belts as well. As for work in the theatre, it seemed that any production being put together would only have a cast of no more than four characters, and probably, only one set. Things began to look very bleak, not just for me, but everyone.

Now, one Monday morning, Ann and I are having our usual morning cup of tea in bed, when the post arrived. I go and collect it and pass it over (for some reason, Ann always opened the post. I can't think why). The first one off the pile is from the Bank. She opens it, and reads, without saying a word, then passes it over to me. It read. "Mr Lyons" not "Dear Mr Lyons", or "Dear John", just "Mr Lyons" "You owe the Bank twenty-nine thousand pounds, what are you doing about it?" They are not the exact words, but close.

John Lyons

We look at each other, then silence. Finally, Ann says, "How are we going to get out of this?" I stopped, looked out of the bedroom window for a minute or so, then turning back said,

"Well, the only way out of this is, I've got to get a television series." Two weeks later, I got a television series that was to last for the next seventeen and a half years. Which was of course, "A TOUCH OF FROST". Somebody up there was listening.

Chapter Twenty: Come Along George, Chop-Chop

It all started for me, with a call from dear Marilyn Johnson to my agent. This was the casting agent, who over the years had given me so much work. "Would John like to come along to Yorkshire Television's Office in Holborn to audition for a new police drama starring David Jason?"

I got the time, and the address, and as usual, was knocking on their door fifteen minutes early. This audition turned out to be not the usual set-up. David himself wasn't present, nor were the writers or the casting department. The people who would normally be in attendance. It was just me, and the producer/director, Don Leaver. Don had just completed producing "Prime Suspect" with Helen Mirren, an enormous success on TV. He would now, not only produce this new drama series, but would direct every fourth episode.

Strangely, he didn't ask me to read, which is in itself unusual, or even tell me what part I was up for. We just sat on either side of the desk, over a cup of coffee, and chatted. Fifty minutes or so pass, when he stood up, shook my hand, and said, "John, welcome to the Thames Valley Police". What he was doing was judging my personality to see if it would not only fit the part, but also, if I would fit in alongside Mr Jason.

An unusual way to conduct an interview, perhaps, but it worked. The part was to be Detective Sergeant George Toolan. The way the show came about, as I was to find out later, occurred at the start of the very last episode of "Darling Buds of May", one of television's biggest hits, and of course, starring David Jason.

During a small break in filming, the producers had taken David out for dinner, and during that evening, asked if he had any thoughts as to what he would like to do next. Well, yes, he had. He, like most of the country, was very much into police dramas. Especially the two-hour version, like "Midsomer Murders", or more to the point, "Morse". Two-hour dramas, where you had time to tell a well-developed story.

That set the ball in motion. Excelsior Productions, who would co-produce alongside Yorkshire TV, began a search for the right vehicle. This took quite a bit of time and quite a bit of reading. Until finally, they came up with three books written by an author by the name of "R.D. Wingfield" called "A Touch of Frost".

After completing a deal with Mr Wingfield's agent, the three books were given over to the brilliant screenwriter Richard Harris who, after quite a bit of work, produced three excellent two-hour episodes. And that's as far as it went. Three episodes.

The filming for those first three episodes began at the beginning of February 1992 and went out on air in December of that year. Once they were filmed and edited, ready for transmission, David himself began to become slightly anxious and worried. Although he himself had seen all three episodes alongside the producers, and all knew that they were more than good, the actor in David now began to worry how the public would accept him, playing the part of a dour scruffy Police Inspector, dealing with subjects involving, murder, missing children, rape etc., after so many years playing mainly, but not all, comedy. Would they accept him?

Not Just George

Well, when the first episode went out on that Sunday in December, all fears vanished. The newspapers, and the public, gave it a large thumbs up. Overnight it went straight to the top of the viewing figures, above even "Coronation Street", which at that time was unheard of. If you were to read any of those three books now, you wouldn't find my character, "George Toolan", anywhere. At that time, he didn't exist.

The screenwriter, Richard Harris, had taken dialogue from other characters in the books and invented "George". The name itself belonged to a chap he played golf with. So, "George Toolan" was born on a golf course in Epsom. I often wonder if the real Mr Toolan was aware of that when he would watch an episode? I hope he was. And I hope he was pleased. Our very first day was the read-through at the BBC rehearsal rooms in Acton.

Everyone of any importance was present, producers, cast, make-up, wardrobe, and of course Mr Jason himself. This was the second time I had met David, the first being in the make-up room at the ATV Studios in Elstree. We sat next to each other and chatted for a while. Little did I know that we would spend many a time sitting next to each other in make-up in the years to come.

On that very first day, Don Leaver (the producer) asked me if I had ever grown a moustache. If not, "Would I let my top lip flourish by the time my first day's filming came around?" which would not be for a month's time. Well, I let my top lip do its own thing. Then, on the day of filming, I presented both myself, and my fully grown moustache to Don.

He was in favour but suggested that as David himself would have a tache in the series, I should present myself to him for his approval. So, I duly knocked on his trailer door and entered. "David, I've been asked to show you my tache for your approval. What do you think?"

He looked twice and said, "Yes, go on, you soppy old sod, you look daft enough", And I've had it ever since.

In our house, my moustache is known as GEORGE. The first scene I would film would be with David, set in a caravan studying maps. I thought about my character for quite a while and the relationship he would have with Frost. I worked on the basis that he had known and worked under him for many years and knew the way, not only how he worked, but how he thought. George may not have agreed with his methods but knew that nine times out of ten, he was right in the end.

Within that scene, Frost quite rightly had the brunt of the dialogue. So, the only way I could create a relationship between Frost and Toolan was through one of an actor's main tools, attitude, looks, body language etc. The very next day, Don Leaver says to me, "Very good work yesterday, John, I saw the rushes this morning, very good." So, I knew I was on the right track.

I'm glad to say that not only had he noticed that there was a relationship possible between these two characters, but also the other two producers, the writers, and most importantly, David himself. From the very beginning, in the early stages of preparing for the series, they had all agreed that Frost would not have a permanent sidekick for a couple of reasons. First, they didn't want it to look too much like "Morse" or "Midsummer Murders", which both had loyal sidekicks. Secondly, if they could introduce other characters along the way, who would appear in maybe one or two episodes, the writers would have more scope for storylines. And for the first four series, that's what happened. The public was introduced to women sidekicks, black sidekicks, even one who was older than Frost. But dear George was always present.

Slowly but surely, as the years went on, because, I think, of the relationship we had developed between the two characters, and the close relationship I had personally with David, George became, without much notice, his trusted friend and sidekick. Not only was Toolan a friend, who at times covered up for him, but in the very last episode, he would ask George to be the best man at his wedding.

Now, I hope I'm not going to spoil the end for anyone who has not seen the very last episode. If so, skip the next paragraph. The last three scenes of the last episode were filmed with three different endings. One of the three main characters, FROST/TOOLAN/ or Superintendent MULLET, played brilliantly by my dear friend Bruce Alexander, an actor blessed with first-class timing, were to be killed off. That scene had all three characters sitting in a car outside a church, where Frost was about to be married.

Opposite, in a large Range Rover, sat the drunken ex-husband of the woman Frost was about to marry. Before we had time to exit the car, he drove at high speed, full-on, into our vehicle. It then cuts to the three of us (filmed one at a time) critically ill in hospital, ending in one of us dying. Then came the very last scene, the funerals of all three. So, now they have three different endings from which they can choose who should die in the can. This particular episode was four hours long, as opposed to the normal two.

The first went out on the Sunday night, the second, and last, the next day, Monday. The decision as to who would go was made on that last day in the hope that the newspapers would not spoil it. I, myself, watched the Sunday episode, but I had to miss the Monday one because I was appearing in a play in the West End. By the time I arrived home, it had already finished ten minutes before. Knowing my wife had been watching, I went up to the lounge, and there she was, tears running down her cheeks.

John Lyons

So, I knew it had been GOODBYE GEORGE. Over almost fifty-nine years as an actor, I have worked on many different shows and enjoyed almost all of them, not all, but most. But none more than "A Touch of Frost". The credit for making this such an enjoyable show to work on must go down to our leading man, Sir David Jason. For me, I think he must be the most generous actor I've ever worked with.

Although he was the leading man, plus one of the executive producers, he didn't necessarily want to have all the dialogue and hog the screen. He much preferred to make it an ensemble piece. There were quite a few occasions when he would give me chunks of his dialogue. Not many leading actors would do that. In fact, I have worked in television with a leading actor, who, very slowly, would have some of my dialogue in quiet conversations with the director, whittled down so that he would dominate the screen. But not David. He wanted everyone working on the show to be a part of it, wardrobe, make-up, lighting, all departments. He liked the idea of a happy family atmosphere.

In any place of work, if everyone is happy and feeling part of it, not just a worker, you get better results. Makes sense. And I, without knowing it, contributed to that feeling. This is how it came about. The storyline had Frost and Toolan walking along a railway track looking for any signs of evidence for a man who had been hit by a train. That was the scene. At a given point, I stop and say,

"Wait a minute, Jack, I think I see a man's finger under that piece of cloth."

"Pick it up" says he, I look, "Go on, pick it up and bag it."

I bend down, remove the cloth, pick it up with tweezers, and bag it. End of scene. The director says, "Lovely, let's go for a take. Oh John, you're wanted in make-up."

I go into make-up. While I'm in there, David has replaced

that false finger with a rather large Cumberland sausage. Out I come. Right, take your positions. Good, sound running, camera running, action.

"Wait a minute, Jack, I think I see a finger under that cloth."

"Pick it up, go on, pick it up and bag it."

I bend down, pull away the cloth, and jump six feet in the air. "Oh, my word" (or words to that effect). I look around, and everyone is doubled up with laughter, including Mr Jason, who has tears running down his face.

Now, this is where I made my mistake. I said, "David, you'll never catch me like that again".

He said, "Do you want a bet?"

"Yes." I say, "How much?"

He replies, "Fifty pounds," with confidence.

"You're on", and we shake.

For the next sixteen years, they found a different wind-up for every episode. They become known as the GEORGE TOOLAN WIND-UPS. They got together some beauties. Here's just a few.

I got a script in which Toolan had a full page and a half speech, explaining to Frost what has happened. I learnt it, rehearsed it, and then filmed it. It didn't exist. I was stopped, after only ten lines in, by the director Paul Harrison, walking in with a board saying, you owe David, FIFTY POUNDS.

On another occasion, I spent one hour in an empty University, looking for the film unit that I had been told was on the second floor, when in fact, they had all left two hours ago. I spent that hour going up and down stairs, looking in every office with no luck, quietly swearing to myself. All of that was captured on the security cameras, which they all had great delight in laughing at the next morning.

One that I, myself, did find particularly funny, is when they dug out an old photograph of me, had it blown up, and then pasted on to the back of a Leeds City bus, with the caption, IF ANYONE SEES THIS MAN IMPERSONATING AN ACTOR, PLEASE CALL THE POLICE. That bus spent two hours driving around Leeds City Centre. I'm glad to say, nobody called the police.

These three examples are only three of many, which had the input of not only David but other members from all departments. So, although it may have cost me a few quid, it was worth it. Which means, that at the age of seventy-eight I still have to work.

I believe, if you wish, you can find some of those out-takes on Youtube. It may have looked a bit hard and unfair to play tricks on me like that, but I took it as a backhanded compliment. You would not play games on an actor like that, while in the middle of filming, if you didn't know that he was a confident, grounded actor who could hold his own. And believe me, I did. A lot of actors would not have been very happy.

You may wonder why that bus with my enlarged photo pasted on the back toured Leeds City Centre? Well, that's where we were based for six months of every year. Alongside Excelsior, the production company, Yorkshire Television provided all the facilities. Therefore, that's where we filmed, and where Ann and I lived for six months, on and off, for seventeen and a half years. Leeds. Over those years, we came to enjoy living in Yorkshire, and would often, on weekends, when not filming, catch a train from the main station, and tour the surrounding countryside. Beautiful.

One long bank holiday weekend, we took the opportunity

to spend it in a lovely small hotel in the Cotswolds. On the first morning, after breakfast, we both decided to go for a walk around this beautiful county.

As we walked out of the front doors, I stopped Ann and said, "Did you see the man sitting in the passenger seat of that car?"

No, she hadn't. "I'm sure it was Paul McCartney," I said, and then forgot about it.

Come the afternoon, after a small lunch, we go for a swim in the hotel's lovely indoor swimming pool. After completing a couple of lengths of the pool, I take a short break, resting against the steps, when I had to make way for a man coming down. As he said a thank you, I turned to face him, and there I stood, face to face, with one of the most famous people in the world: Sir Paul McCartney. Without thinking, I said, "Hi Paul, how are you?" and shook his hand as if I had known him for years. Well, he did, in turn, return my handshake, and we spoke for a few minutes or so before I said, "Lovely to meet you," and swam off.

I noticed he had his family with him, and of course, he got this all the time. Fifteen minutes go by, and I pull myself up and sit on the side of the pool, with my legs dangling in the water. When all of a sudden, Sir Paul swims over, pulls himself up alongside me, and asks, "How's Sir David Jason?"

Well, well, he knows who I am. But then, why not. Everyone watches TV at some time. We spend the next five minutes or so talking about other people we have in common. One of them being Junior Campbell, founder of the pop group, "Marmalade" (The Beatles had written "OB LA DI, OB LA DA" and given it to the group, which went on to become their biggest hit).

When along comes his daughter Stella, and says, "Dad, we have to go."

We say our goodbyes, and off they go. I cannot tell you, my friends, what a lovely, friendly, normal person, Sir Paul is, and so talented. One week later, I'm telling Sir David that Sir Paul was asking after him, and he was chuffed. Why not? We all have our heroes.

At the start of each episode, we would spend one week rehearsing in London, which meant that all actors in that particular episode were able to attend when they got their calls. After that, David, Bruce and I would travel up to Leeds, ready for the first day on Monday. Bruce, playing "Mullet" or "Horned Rimmed Harry" as "Frost" would later call him, would not necessarily be called until all the office scenes were to be filmed. But, for "George" I would often be there for the whole five weeks of filming.

The thinking behind this was, that as the Sergeant to Frost's Inspector, if, for some reason, something went wrong, like weather, or David himself had to be somewhere else that day, or even if he were to wake up one morning feeling poorly, "George" as his second in command, could legitimately take over.

This, of course, would mean that I would have to be fairly well up on Frost's dialogue. But I'm pleased to say I only had to save the day on two occasions in all those years. I often think back, with great pleasure, on all the first-class actors that joined us throughout those years. Many unknown, but all excellent, and some that are now household names. Damian Lewis, Marc Warren, Cherie Lunghi and a very young talented Danny Dyer, to name but a few.

Apart from the first-class writers, who produced gripping storylines, our team of producers and directors were top drawer—Roger Bamford, Paul Harrison, and of course David Reynolds. I myself have always enjoyed watching other actors work, even amateur ones, that may sound strange, but sometimes watching bad acting can show you how not to do it. (I hope that doesn't sound too rude?) I would always, with the second director's permission, and of course, the actors, sit in on a rehearsal, whether or not I was in that particular scene. Fascinated how other actors worked on a scene. (You're never too late to learn new things).

Not only did I watch David in rehearsal, but got to play many scenes with him and watched the way he worked close up. I myself, having a long list of TV credits behind me, knew the old saying, "Less is always better on camera." It is very true. But being so close up to him in a scene, it seemed as though it wasn't acting at all. Which, in the end, is the objective? His face would sometimes tell the audience what he was thinking without having to say a word. Plus, for me, a very important part of acting, a great ability to listen.

That may sound a silly and easy thing to do. But most of the time, whilst the first actor is talking. You can see the other one desperately trying to think of their next line. The glazing over of the eyes is a sure sign, which tells you that the actor is not really in the scene. The ability to listen is very powerful, not only on screen but also very much so on stage. Watch Anthony Hopkins, a master of the craft. This ends today's acting class.

One of the many things that David did that took me by surprise was, first thing in the morning when we would run the first scene of the day, he would still have his script with him. If there were three or four other actors in that same scene, we would all be off the book. We would run it two or maybe three times until the director or the director of photography gave his estimate as to how long he would need to light the set. Now, we could all return to our dressing rooms and wait to be called. This happened on every occasion.

After a month went by, and I began to get to know David a little bit more, I asked him what the idea was for him to have his script with him at that first run-through? His explanation was that he had learnt the scene almost ninety per cent and left the rest until after he had seen what the other actors in that scene would bring to it. Then, when we were released for half an hour or so, he would bone up on the other ten per cent, incorporating what he had gathered from the other actors in that first run through, which could possibly change the way he was thinking. Clever and unusual.

One of the other interesting elements of great interest to me was how, over time, he went about building a character. He would invent little bits of character business that the writer could not write. Only the actor could fill those gaps. Things that seem very small, like opening his drawer, and we see a half-eaten burger. Or when, in the middle of a speech, he would take my coffee or pinched my chips. But the one I found most amusing was when he took down a statement or read out an official police charge, he would read it from an old envelope that had been in his pocket for ages.

David, very much like that other first-class actor John Thaw, was a very private person. David in particular. Back in 2005, a gold embossed invitation arrived at home, with a covering letter saying that, on the first of December, our dear Queen will perform the ceremony of turning Mr David Jason OBE, the boy from Finchley, into Sir David Jason. It went on. Both Gill and I would like you both very much to join us and our family for a celebration lunch at the Dorchester Hotel. Please R.S.V.P. Also, please keep this under your hat.

Well, we both put on our finest clobber, and were on our best behaviour. What we didn't know, was that the night before, David and Gill had got married in a private suite at the Dorchester, with just his brother Arthur, sister June, and their respective spouses, plus Gill's mother and brother present—not forgetting their young daughter Sophie. Now, anyone else in showbiz would have had OK magazine, or HELLO magazine, who not only would have given it a lot of publicity but would have paid for the whole day. But not David. He valued his privacy too much. Plus, like John Thaw, they didn't need the publicity. Their work spoke for them.

At one point, between episodes of "FROST", Ann and I, with our daughter, took a week's holiday down in Bournemouth. At the end of that week, while preparing to drive back to London, Ann suggested, perhaps we could take a look at a lodge that was up for sale in a beautiful part of the New Forest.

We had looked at this lodge two months previously, and, as it was on our way home, it wouldn't be too much out of our way. When we got there, surely enough, it still had the "For Sale" notice up.

"Just out of interest, why not find out what they want for it," says my wife. (I think she had planned this). The land and the eight lodges that were on it, all situated around a small stream, was owned, at that time, by a rather wealthy farmer. We did indeed enquire at the small office, got the relevant information, and carried on homewards. Of course, that became the only topic of conversation for the whole journey.

Two days later, I'm back up in Leeds to resume filming and sitting in David's trailer having a cup of tea. In conversation I tell him that Ann and I had seen this lovely lodge at the weekend, set in a beautiful spot, on the edge of the New Forest. "I'm in two minds whether or not I should buy it, what do you think?"

He said, "Buy it, buy it and call it Repeat Villas." I did, and he was right. The repeats did in fact pay for it. Clever old sausage. We spent some lovely times down there, walking in the forest, along the cliff top overlooking the sea, barbecues with our lovely neighbours, Roy and Margaret Weeks, plus having long term friends, Cheryl and Derek Masters visit at weekends.

Although I owned the lodge outright, I didn't own the land it stood on. So, when my ten-year lease was up and due for renewal, the owner, who knew he had me by the short and *****, put the ground rent up two-fold. He knew there was no way I would have the whole lodge unplumbed, hire a crane and a lorry, and find another site. So reluctantly, I sold it back to him. You can bet your boots, he sold it on again, making a "nice little earner", as Del boy would say. Great shame. Had that farmer not been so greedy, Ann and I would still be there today.

Around this time, I started to feel unwell. In fact, I had been feeling unwell for quite a few months whilst filming "Frost" with pains in the stomach. But, like most men, we think it will go away, and we do nothing. Stupid. Eventually, it got so bad that one morning Ann gave up on me and called an ambulance. Thank you, wife.

It turned out, I had three large stones in my gall bladder. The consultant later told me, if I had left it any longer, it could have passed into the pancreas, and that would have been my final curtain. I was admitted straight away, had X-rays, and two days later, an operation. For the next ten days, I lay in a hospital bed, with tubes coming out of every orifice, unable to eat or drink. One evening both Ann and my daughter Laura come to visit. Now. I don't know if you are aware, but Consultants are not called Doctor, just Mister. My Consultant is Mr Ham.

At the end of the visit, we say our goodbyes, and my girls go to leave. Laura stops in the doorway, turns and says, "Dad, have you looked on the wall behind you?" I slowly turn around and see JOHN LYONS. HAM. I look back, and just as she goes out, she says, "I think that about sums you up". Cheeky. But probably right.

One of the nice things about being in a very popular TV series is people recognising you and talking to you, anywhere, anytime. Quite a few people over the years have said to me "Don't you get fed up with people keep coming up and talking to you?"

Well, no, I don't. Because almost everyone who does has always been very nice and complimentary. Except one who comes to mind. I'm walking down a large market, close to where I live, when on the opposite side of the road is a fella in his forties, with his old, and I guess deaf mum, going the other way. He stops, clocks me, and in a very loud voice that could have been heard in Southend, says, "Mum, look, there he is, that's that fucking geezer off the telly."

Well, I'm not easily embarrassed, but in this case, I put my head down and made a very quick exit. That night over dinner, I tell the story to both my wife and my daughter, leaving out, of course, the F word. Four days later, I'm back up in Leeds and phone home.

Laura, my daughter, who at this time is only seven years old, answers. We have a five-minute chat, and I say, "Is your mum there?"

"Yeah, hold on…. mum… mum, IT'S THAT GEEZER OFF THE TELLY."

I love her sense of humour. That's how I am known now at home, THE GEEZER OFF THE TELLY.

John Lyons

Ann and I live overlooking a lovely big park in London named Victoria Park, so named after Queen Victoria, who performed the opening ceremony in the early 1800s. One lovely Monday morning in 2005, I'm sitting with a cup of coffee and the daily newspaper on our balcony, which gives a great view over a large part of the park. It's about 10.30 in the morning. Everybody has gone off to work, including Ann, and it's so quiet. You could hear that famous pin drop.

Sitting on a park bench, not too far away, are two lovely old cockney ladies who live at the other end of our road. Now, I don't know, in fact, I don't think anyone knew, that a member of the Royal Family was coming to the park that day, in order to plant a tree, to honour the first planting by Queen Victoria all those years back. It hadn't been advertised or talked about, so nobody was aware that this was happening. I stopped reading for a while, and looking around, I noticed the big park gates to my left were wide open - unusual, first time for ages. I paid no more attention and went back to my newspaper.

Suddenly, through the gates, enter two police outriders on motorcycles, followed by two large black limousines with their tops rolled back. Sitting in the back of the first car, splendid in a large yellow hat and matching dress, is our dear Queen Mother, in deep conversation with her lady-in-waiting. As the cars reached the two old ladies, the Queen Mother, without looking, gave them the Royal wave, and swept on by. Half a minute passes, and all again is quiet. When slowly, one of the lovely old ladies, turned to the other and said, "Who the fucking hell was that?"

Wonderful. It was a pity I was the only one around to witness it.

A very strange happening occurred in the middle of filming "Frost". Outside my front door are our electric and gas meters. One lovely summer's afternoon, two workmen spent a couple of hours outside my door, installing a new meter. I, being the very friendly and trusting person that I am, left the front door open in case they needed anything, even at one point, offering them tea, and left them to it.

The next morning, Ann and I are going out shopping, and I asked her, "Have you seen my wallet?". "It's on the sideboard," Ann said.

"Well, it's not now."

Now, I can't prove or accuse the two workmen, but our sideboard is right inside the front door, which would have been very easy to just take a couple of steps inside, and thank you very much. In that wallet is, of course, not only two credit cards, a debit card, but also my medical card and other personal information.

I did, of course, cancel all of them immediately. An item like this is of great value when being sold on, especially if that person knows your address and roughly what you look like. A month later, I'm at home on the Saturday night with my wife and daughter, when there's a ring on the doorbell.

Laura, my daughter, looks out the window, and says, "Dad, there are two police officers downstairs."

Down I go and answer the door. At this time, I'm in my pyjamas and dressing gown. As I open the door, the two officers, one male, one female, just stare and look at each other. Finally, one says, "Mr Lyons?"

"Yes," I said.

They then look at my house number and again look back at each other.

"What's the problem, officers?"

"Do you have a brother?"

"I do, yes", I replied, "Is there a problem?"

"Could you tell us his name?"

"Of course, Joe," I replied. Once more, they look at each other.

"Officers, this is now getting silly, you are now frightening both my wife and my daughter. You must tell me what the problem is. Has my brother had an accident?"

The woman police officer now goes down the few steps to the pavement and gets on her phone. She's back in a minute or so and shakes her head at the other police officer. Now I have had enough.

I said, "Officers, I need to know what's going on?"

"Okay, Mr Lyons", she said, "I think I can tell you now. This afternoon, from the Regents canal, we recovered a dead body of a man, dressed in a hospital gown, and around his wrist, he had all your details on a hospital wristband."

Now, they have come to inform my wife that her husband is dead, and could she, at the same time, please come to identify the body. This could only have happened if that person had got hold of my details, gone to the hospital, who in turn held all my information, and checked himself in as me. The other, for me, funny part, was when I opened the door, dressed in pyjamas and dressing gown, the two officers took a step back and looked at each other. They must have thought, "That Mrs Lyons is a bit quick, her husband's only been dead a few hours, and already she's shacked up with someone else."

We were so shocked. I completely forgot to ask which station they came from so that I could follow it up. The very next day, I leave to go up to Leeds, to start filming again on the Monday. During that day, David and I are having coffee, and I tell him that story. "Wait a minute, wait a minute," he says. "Come into my dressing room." He gets out his typewriter and says, "Tell me that again."

I did, he typed it out, we cleaned it up, and sold it to the production company, who in turn, passed it on to a professional screenwriter who turned it into a very good episode of "Frost". It`s called "DEAD MALE ONE"—a true story.

Chapter Twenty-One:
Back on The Boards

Four years after finishing "Frost", David brought his family down to Worthing in Sussex, where I was appearing in panto with Amanda Barrie. After the show we all went for dinner, and David and I began reminiscing over "A Touch of Frost".

I said to him "I do miss it, you know?"

He replied, "So do I."

"Couldn't we just make one more?" I asked.

"No, I'm too old, and you're dead."

I suppose that just about sums it up. Once the series was over and done with, I went to have a chat with my agent at the time, June Epstein. After seventeen and a half years of TV work, and hopefully, many years of repeat showings to come, we both agreed that theatre would be our next best bet. Something that I myself would be more than happy to do.

So, June set about making enquiries. The first thing she came up with was "A Woman in Black". Well, I go along to see it, and I'm slightly in shock. It's a great play, with many a twist and turn, but it only had two characters in the whole play, which frightened the life out of me. At this moment in time, I had not been on stage for eighteen years, so the thought of learning all those lines, and performing them eight times a week for twelve months, made me come out in a cold sweat.

No, what I needed was a play where the part was enough to keep me busy, not the leading part, and with not so many lines. Next, she came up with the world's longest-running play "The Mousetrap". Ah, sounds good. I go along to meet the director, and then watch a performance. Lovely, just what I'm looking for. A play where I could hide away and see if I still had the dedication to be in a long run.

The part is dear old "Major Metcalf". He has five entrances throughout the play, with just enough dialogue to keep me happy, and not tire me out. Because this will be a twelve-month run. Can you see a pattern here, of how an actor's mind works as he gets older? When young and keen, he wants as many lines and entrances as possible. Now, he starts to look for the easy route.

The other factor in taking this job means that I can live at home, which after being away in Leeds for so long, was a bonus. I could leave my house and be in the West End dressing room in forty-five minutes. Not only did I accept the job, but I went on to repeat it twice more with a five-year gap between each one. Notching up a total of one thousand two hundred performances. (I'm tired just thinking of that figure.)

"The Mousetrap" itself is a strange old warhorse, opening in 1952, at the Ambassadors Theatre for the first six years, then, when the St Martins Theatre next door became available, which is a much bigger theatre, it moved there, and that's where it stays to this day. And who knows, forever. I always found it amazing how many people would come to the stage door most nights, wanting to chat. We would, of course, get a lot of tourists, Japanese, Chinese, people from the low countries, Belgium, Holland etc. Their comments were nearly always, "We come to see this play because we are learning English, and you all speak perfect English, with no slang or swear words. (They should have heard me before I went to drama school. I could have taught them a few swear words.)

The other visitors were Americans. The comment most often heard there was, "My grandmother saw it. My mother saw it. Now it's my turn." It was as though they passed it down from generation to generation. Over the years, it became one of the sights to see when coming to London, alongside Tower Bridge, Big Ben, and Buckingham Palace.

Amazing, considering no one expected it to run for more than six months back in 1952. It's a fact that the play had been turned down by at least two directors, before being taken up by the director, Peter Coates. It obviously helped by having as its leading man, Richard Attenborough.

There are many drawbacks in being in a long-running play - one of the most important being concentration. When you're repeating the same dialogue every night, and listening to the same coming back at you, you have to be on the ball at all times. It may not be you who makes the mistake, but the other actor. Therefore it would be up to you to get the scene back on track.

During the whole run, over three different years, with three different casts, I only dried once. But it was a beauty. Of course, it would have to happen in the very last scene of the play, when I, as the "Major", sum up the whole plot. It was like hitting a brick wall. My mind went completely blank. I could not think of one single word. There I stood in the middle of the stage, with the rest of the cast staring at me, but unable to help. Even to this day, I still have no idea of what I said or how I got off, but I'm sure it didn't make any sense to that audience. It never happened again.

Not Just George

The only other mistake I made during my time there was unforgivable. It was something an actor should never let happen. I MISSED AN ENTRANCE. Leaving two actors on stage alone after they had finished their dialogue, waiting for me to enter. It really wasn't my fault, but I did take the blame. Behind the set and through a back door, there is what's known as a Green Room. A room where the actors can sit, maybe have a cup of tea while waiting for their next entrance.

Up on the wall is a speaker so that everyone is able to follow what place they have reached on stage. This particular evening, I'm sitting, with a cuppa, chatting to a female member of the cast, whilst at the same time, keeping half an ear cocked on the speaker. As it reached a certain point, where I would normally put the cup in the sink and make my way to the side of the stage, my chatty female friend asked me another question. Like a fool, and without thinking, I sat down again and began to answer. One minute must have passed when the door flew open, and the stage manager hissed the words that no actor ever wants to hear. "JOHN, YOU'RE ON."

Well, of course, I ran, heart racing, to the side of the stage, where I would make my very late entrance. Let me set the scene on stage for you. Just two actors. One, the lady of the house, who has, of course, by now run out of dialogue, and a gentleman house guest, who likewise has been struck dumb. She picks up a tea cloth and begins a little light dusting of the bookcase. He (my dear gay friend David) goes over to the fireplace, picks up the poker, and starts to poke the fire. I take a deep breath, enter, and begin speaking.

Now, all three of us will not look at each other, knowing if we do, the giggles will start. I have no idea how we got to the end of the scene, but we did, and all three made our

146

exit together. When we got to the safety of the wings, I, of course, cannot apologise enough.

"No, no, my dear boy," says David.

"But David, I just left you alone on stage, for about a minute and a half."

"No, don`t worry. I thank you."

"You thank me, why?"

"That's the longest poke I've ever had."

Oh well, that's showbiz. I learnt my lesson. CONCEN-TRATE. Over the years, "The Mousetrap" has had many famous visitors. Tom Hanks, Dustin Hoffman, and many members of Government, and the Royal Family. Our dear late Queen Mother, Princess Margaret, and on at least three occasions over those years, the Queen herself, accompanied by Prince Phillip.

On the occasion of the play's fiftieth year, it became a Royal event. The Queen and the Prince would attend a Gala Performance. At that time, I had finished my stint in the show, but the management very kindly invited both Ann and me, along with other past members of previous casts, to attend. There we were, me all done up in an evening suit, with a very colourful bow tie, Ann, dressed up to the nines, sitting in prime position in the dress circle.

I took the aisle seat, as I often did, to be able to stretch the old legs when need be. When Her Majesty and the Prince enter at the back of the dress circle, we all stand. They start to make their way down the steps heading for the front row, when suddenly the Prince stops, looks at me, then comes over for a quick chat.

I can't remember exactly what was said, something on the lines of, "How are you, have you seen this play before?" etc.

I do remember telling him that "Yes, I have been in three previous productions." With that, he left and joined the Queen in their front row seats. When the first act interval arrived, we all stood again, whist they both made their way up the stairs, heading, I guess for the bar.

Once again, the Prince comes over and asks me what I think of the performances? This time Her Majesty herself joins him. She doesn`t speak but gives me a most wonderful smile, and they both head off, surrounded by dignitaries. By now, the row we are sitting in is all leaning forward and making various comments.

"You have a new friend there, Johnny boy."

"Get his autograph next time", and so on.

Here they come again, surely not this time? Oh yes. "Is it still the same ending?"

"Yes, it is, Sir." He smiles, then off. At the final curtain, when the applause has finished, they head once more up the steps, on their way backstage to meet the cast. My whole row is waiting.

As he passes, he looks over and says, "Very nice to meet you."

"You too, Sir" and he's gone.

"Woooo, get you" is one of the many comments a voice behind me says, "There has to be a knighthood in that somewhere for you, Johnny boy."

For quite a while afterwards, I would get cards from old cast members, asking how my old mate Phil was. Most of them with the title, Sir John on the envelope. I don't know if the Prince thought I was someone else, or he recognised my face, which is quite possible, because, like all families, they also watch television.

John Lyons

Sometime during 2003/4 we were in the middle of one of the runs of "The Mousetrap" when my agent received a call from Marilyn Johnson, asking for my availability for a surprise episode of "Frost". I say a surprise because there was a real probability that David may be calling it a day. I would be required for the full six weeks filming up in Leeds.

This, indeed, would be the last episode, as David had, indeed, decided to call it a day. The story line for this last episode had "Frost" telling "Toolan" to head across a roof in pursuit of a villain while he would be waiting at the other end. In the course of the chase, Toolan would fall from that roof and finish up in hospital, where he would remain for the entire episode, falling in and out of consciousness until finally passing away. He, Frost would take the blame, and, full of guilt, would resign from the force for good. That was to be the plot. Now, at this time, I'm halfway through a run of "The Mousetrap" in London, and the management refused to let me out of my contract for that period.

Sadly, my agent gets back to them to give them the news. A day or so passes when Marilyn comes back with this. "Would it be possible, if the script were to be rewritten, so that Toolan would have a lesser role, but would ultimately survive, could John travel up to Leeds on Saturday nights, after his last performance, film with us all day Sunday, again Monday morning, and we would guarantee to have him back in London by two o'clock Monday afternoon?"

And that is what happened. A car would be waiting for me outside the theatre, have me up into the hotel in Leeds by two o'clock in the morning, I would then film for those two days, and be back in London for Monday night's performance. When the management at "The Mousetrap" refused to grant me leave. I was very disappointed.

In the long run, it worked out, not only to my benefit but

other regular members of the cast, because we went on to make another sixteen episodes over the following six years. For which the ITV network was very happy about. Not only was "Frost" a big success in this country, but many countries around the world.

One of the lovely benefits of being in a very popular TV series is that quite a lot of other work starts to come your way. One of the first was PANTOMIME. Back in my Stratford East days, I must have appeared in at least four. Now, I was being offered, what's known as number one pantos. This was to be "Dick Whittington" starring the comedian Jim Davidson. Jim was not only starring but also directing in his own production.

I had always found that working with a comedian, as I did many times on TV, was, at the beginning, tricky. When you think about it, a comedian spends most of his career working alone, unless, of course, he is part of a double act. But now, he has an actor alongside him. You could almost see it in their eyes. They are thinking, "Can I trust this man?"

Well, I'm glad to say that it only took a couple of days for Jim to realise he could trust me. Once that was established, he very quickly began to play around and improvise with me in scenes, knowing that not only would I not be thrown, but that I would come back with a line or two of my own. That would lead him into further improvisation. I did enjoy those scenes, standing on a stage with a top comedian, in front of an audience, sometimes of two thousand, and to hear a wave of laughter roll over you. It's something most actors don't normally experience. Wonderful.

I got on very well with Mr Davidson, and I think I worked very well with him. I must have done because I went on to appear in another six pantomimes, alongside both him and his TV partner, the snooker player John Virgo. We played some of the biggest theatres in the country, starting at the

John Lyons

Palace Theatre Manchester and taking in Bristol Hippodrome, the Mayflower Southampton, and many more.

The one theatre I do remember very well is the Derngate Theatre Northampton, for two reasons: as the interval approached to end the first act of the matinee performance, the cast boarded the ship that would take us off to Morocco, all singing and waving to the audience. The ship itself was balanced on a series of runners, which, on cue, was pulled into the wings by four big hairy stagehands as the curtain fell. This had been performed many times before without a problem.

This time however, before it could reach the safety of the wings, it slipped off the runners and came to a sudden halt. I, being the first on board and with my back to the wings, suddenly found myself flying through the air, backwards, with John Virgo a close second. Crash, I hit the stage floor head first, followed by J.V. landing on top of me. And if you can picture him. He's a biggun. I must have been knocked out for a few minutes, because when I finally opened my eyes, people, including a St Johns ambulance man, were bending over me.

What made me giggle later on was, as I looked to the left, there was Mr Davidson pacing up and down. When he saw me open my eyes, he rushed over, bent down, and kissed me full on the lips. Then uttered the immortal words, "Thank God love, I thought you were Brown Bread." He was thinking of the INSURANCE. The next thing I knew was both John and I being taken out of the stage door on stretchers. What the patients, sitting in the A & E department of Northampton General thought, when they saw two silly old actors, in full medieval costume and make up, being carried through, heaven only knows.

They kept me in until the middle of the night, after they were satisfied I wasn't suffering from concussion. As for dear J.V., he had an x-ray and was sent back to the hotel, feeling very sore, but nothing broken. Both of us missed the second show but were both back the next day. Apparently, for that second show, with two main characters missing, Jim had gone out and improvised the whole of the second act to great applause.

I cut now to three months later, and Ann and I are in a very large superstore in South London. As I'm walking down one of the aisles, around the corner comes a man, who stares at me and then says, "You're John Lyons, oh my word, I was there that night when you got knocked out, were taken to hospital, and Jim made the rest up, oh, that was one of the funniest nights I have ever had."

Oh good, I'm glad he found it amusing. So, as you can tell, pantomimes can be very dangerous places, what with all the set changes, curtains flying in and out, sword fights, not to mention at least twenty-odd children making up the cast. You need to be on your toes at all times. Five days later, during a matinee performance of "Dick Whittington" we were just coming up to the last scene, and I'm taking my place down stage left, when I notice two of the crew carrying away the actor Victor Spinetti who in this production is playing the big role of King Rat.

Victor had been complaining for a few weeks about his ears. Now it seems he is suffering a nasty dizzy spell, and on the verge of collapse. The whole of that last scene is all about King Rat, so, without him, we have a problem. Jim, of course, saves the day by talking to the audience, and ad-libbing.

When the curtain finally comes down, everyone is asked to go to Jim's dressing room for a meeting. This is what happened next. He says, "As you all can see, Victor has been taken off to hospital, and will not be back for the evening performance. We have a full house tonight, and by now, they are all on their way, so the show cannot be cancelled. So, there's only one way out of this, John Lyons. You have to play both parts."

"WHAT" says I.

"Think about it," he says. "Your character, the Alderman, only meets King Rat in the last scene. When we get to that, we can all make it up."

"Ah, wait a minute, wait a minute, the opening of the second act, King Rat has that big rap song with all the kids, I can't learn that in an hour."

"Don't worry. I've got that on click track" (tape). He's got me. "We will have a dresser on each side to help you change costumes, and if you need it, a script."

"You're dead right, I'll need it. OK, of course, I'll do it, but everyone else in the cast must come along with me. If I go wrong, and I will believe me, and you don't get the right cue, please don't stand there looking at me, HELP me out."

We now have half an hour to set props, scripts, and anything else I might need in both wings before we go up. When that curtain goes up, I, as King Rat, will be the first thing they see in my rat's lair. The overture starts up, and I can hear the audience buzzing. What I had forgotten was that Ann and my daughter Laura were in the audience that night. Apparently, they had been trying to get through to me, without success, so had not the slightest idea what was about to happen.

Whilst the music was playing, Jim came over and said, "John boy, just enjoy yourself, I know I will." Then, clever lad that he is, he got onto the front of house microphone and made this announcement to the audience. "Ladies and Gentlemen, unfortunately, Mr Victor Spinetti, who plays the part of King Rat, is indisposed, so will not be appearing this evening. Therefore, Mr John Lyons, who plays the part of Alderman Fitzwarren, will tonight play both parts. The problem is, he only knows ONE!"

Wonderful, big laugh, now, even before the curtain goes up, the audience is in on the joke. They are on my side. I made quite a few mistakes that night, went on with the wrong hat, etc., but it didn't matter, panto audiences love it when things go wrong. By the time we got to the walk down at the end, Jim insisted I entered last (a place that is reserved for the top of the bill).

That night, for the first time in my life, I got a standing ovation, not only from the audience but the rest of the cast and all of the crew—a very special moment.

One lasting memory I have of Northampton is the lovely cottage that we took for the duration of the run, next door to Althorp House, the childhood home, and last resting place of Princess Diana. We were joined for Christmas and the New Year by our good friends Cheryl and Derek Masters. A lovely time, but you won't be surprised to learn that I have given Northampton a wide berth ever since.

Pantomimes have played a big and very enjoyable part of my life. A lot of actors are very wary about playing in panto, for quite a few, it frightens them. To start with, you have to be a little bit of an extrovert, a bit of a show-off, someone who is not afraid to make a fool of himself. I'm all of those.

In the normal career of a stage actor, when performing in a play, you have what's known as the fourth wall between you and the audience. When in panto, or a musical, that invisible wall disappears, and you have to face out-front and confront the audience. That audience is as much a part of the show as the performers on stage. Without them, you don't have a show.

John Lyons

You yourself have to feel confident, free, and ready for anything because you are going to get some sort of involvement, at some point, from certain members of that audience. In the form of one or two calling out, which can't be ignored, kids crying, or mums having to take them out in the middle of your speech, to the toilet. Plus, certain things do at some point, go wrong. An actor forgets his lines, a problem with a prop, or the set, or an actor is forced to ad-lib.

All these things do happen, and when they do, the audience loves it. They love to see things go wrong. I'll let you into a little secret. Most of it is planned and rehearsed. BUT DON'T TELL THE KIDS. So, for most actors, the prospect of having to cope with all that twice a day, six days a week, is not their idea of how to spend the festive season. For me, I love it. I love the freedom it gives me.

It's probably the only time of the year when you get the chance to join in songs, dances, and comedy sketches. Sketches that have been performed by some wonderful, long gone comics. After finishing those seven first-class pantos with Jim Davidson, I was asked to go along and meet the producers of Paul Holman Associates at their offices in Ruislip. It was there I first met both Paul Holman, and his partner John Ogle. Instantly we all got on very well together and still do to this day.

PHA, as it's known, is a production company that has been providing not only pantomimes but other forms of entertainment all over the country for well over twenty-five years. For the last fifteen years, I've worked for them in twelve pantos all over the country. The first being Captain Hook in Peter Pan up in Telford. Followed by Aladdin, Sleeping Beauty, Cinderella, Jack and the Beanstalk and a few more, all in lovely theatres throughout the land.

Both Ann and I have had great fun, and lots of wonderful

memories, of all the people we have met, and worked with over those years. To name a few - Chesney Hawkes (the one and only) Amanda Barrie, (Coronation Street), the TV chef, Rusty Lee, Didi Conn (she played Frenchy in the film Grease), Marina Sirkis (Star Trek) and many more. Paul himself will often call for a chat throughout the year but will always call me in the summer to tell me where he would like me to appear that year.

Whatever the panto is going to be, he always lets me know what would be expected of me in that show. If, for instance, it involves the sketch, "Twelve Days of Christmas", that could prove a bit energetic for an old actor like me. If so, they would change it. That's how they think and how they look after me. Lovely. You can see why I've been very happy to work for them all these years.

Whilst performing in a Paul Holman panto at the Broadway Theatre, Catford, a musical director/producer, came along one night and asked if I would kindly join both him and his wife for a drink in the theatre bar after the show. The purpose of this little meeting was to offer me the part of "Sir Joseph Porter" in Gilbert and Sullivan's 'HMS Pinafore.'

Well, what a lovely surprise. I was greatly flattered. I had, over the years, seen a few productions of Gilbert and Sullivan but never appeared in one. This part called for not only acting, a little dancing but mainly the songs of Gilbert and Sullivan, which, believe me, are not easy. This production was to take place on board a boat, moored on the River Thames at Henley. It would have a full cast and orchestra, and the audience would be situated on the vast sloping bank in front with the option to bring a picnic if desired.

It didn't take me long to make a decision. If they could agree to terms with Patsy Martin, my Agent, I would love to be involved. Dates and money had been agreed upon, and we would open in the middle of August that very same year. The acting part went in quite quickly, but it wasn't easy learning those songs. These kinds of songs, and the way of singing them, was new to me, but after a few weeks, I had that very fast patter delivery in my head. Now I was beginning to enjoy myself and greatly looking forward to having a chance to do something completely different.

We reached the end of May, and all came tumbling down. Apparently, the company who was putting up the money had looked ahead to the long-range weather forecast for August, got cold feet, and pulled the plug on the whole venture. They did, to their credit, pay me a fee for the work I had done, but it wasn't the same. I wanted to do it—a great disappointment. Of course, when August came around, the weather could not have been nicer. I think Ann was more disappointed than me. Oh well. Once more, that's showbiz.

Chapter Twenty-Two:
Cruising with P & O

At the time of writing this, we are all in the middle of this awful pandemic, so, not only me, but the whole country has been put on hold. So far this year, I have had two tours of two different plays, postponed, two P & O cruise ships cancelled (I give talks on their ships) and, panto for PHA, which would have been at the Marina Theatre Lowestoft.

That, I'm glad to say, has not been cancelled but postponed until Christmas 2021. When I shall once more give my "Baron Hardup" in Cinderella. "NOT TO BE MISSED". So said the local paper. But then, you can't believe everything you read in the newspapers.

I mentioned just now, P & O cruise ships, on which I give talks, not only about my life but acting in general. All that came about in 2008, when an agent by the name of Patsy Martin, at Personal Appearances, got in touch with my agent at the time, June Epstein, to ask if "John had ever given talks before?"

Well, no, I never had, but I would certainly think about it. If so, Patsy thought she could sell me to P & O as a guest speaker. With the encouragement of my wife (she could see a few holidays coming her way), I did get together not only one talk but three, which could, if need be, last three hours (but not at the same time). I greatly surprised myself.

The first cruise we went on was one of P & O's oldest ship

at the time, "Victoria", sailing along the Italian Adriatic coast. After one week, and thank heavens, I had finished my talks, the weather took a turn for the worse, and I mean a BIG turn. Almost all passengers on board were going down with the dreaded travel sickness. Entertainment onboard was being cancelled, hardly anyone was turning up in the restaurants, and all activities on decks were closed. Both my wife and I were affected badly.

At one point, I looked over to her bunk, and she had tied herself in with blankets, afraid of falling out. My word, it was bad. Silly me, I had forgotten about that awful experience I had whilst filming "The Onedin Line". I should have thought ahead and taken precautions.

After that, we did. When the next cruise came up, we both went to see our doctor, who prescribed tablets that would be compatible with tablets we were both taking for various minor ailments at the time, blood pressure, cholesterol etc. Just in case.

A good move, John and Ann, for as of this moment, and still counting, we have completed thirty-two P & O cruises. What a wonderful job. They not only look after us very well, but we must have travelled around the world at least three times. From Sydney to Peru, from Hawaii to India, from Russia to San Francisco and all points west. I do have to work for my supper, but that's not too much of a hardship would you say?

It goes without saying, Ann, my wife, loves it. Who wouldn't? We made some very good friends along the way, some we still keep in touch with, Clive and Maria, John and Jane, Helen and Shirley, and of course, all the other first-class entertainers we met and worked with onboard ship. The late, incredible magician, Paul Daniels, along with his wife, the lovely Debbie McGee. Wonderful Brian Conley, and Tom O'Connor, a man who can still do two hours stand-up after all these years. All this down to Patsy Martin, at Personal Appearances, who is now my full-time agent. And a great job she does.

Chapter Twenty-Three: Out on Tour

A theatre touring company I was very glad entered my life is Rumpus Theatre, run by John Goodrum, a man who not only acts in some productions but also writes quite a few of them, directs, oversees the lighting, the sets, plus all the touring dates. In other words, an all-round clever clogs.

John had come to see a performance I was in of "The Mousetrap" he hadn't come specifically to see me, but another member of the cast. At the time John had written a new play, based on the story of "Jack the Ripper," and thought that I might be interested in playing the part of the Police Inspector who investigated the case. In due course, he sent the script. I read it and liked it very much. I particularly liked the unusual twist at the end.

We met up, instantly got on very well, and I agreed there and then to be part of it. Once all the details had been finalised and the dates confirmed, I set about learning this rather large part. Luckily, I had a period of three months to get this under my belt. All went well, and after the first month, I nearly had the first act committed to memory. I then ran into a problem.

For the past year, I had been attending our local hospital with a small problem. This was not responding to the treatment I had been having, which meant I would be required to visit them on a more regular basis. I thought about this for a few days, regarding whether I should be leaving London to go off on tour around the country, or, seeing that there were another two and a half months before that tour started, Rumpus would have time to replace me.

Ann and I decided it was more important that I stayed home, and hopefully, get the problem sorted. So, reluctantly, I had to pull out. I'm very glad to say, John understood the situation and very kindly let me out of the contract. They did go off on a successful tour, with a very good actor, David Gilbrook, playing the Inspector. Three years later, Rumpus got in touch once more. This time, John had written a new play based on the character "Father Brown" from the books by G. K. Chesterton, at the time, a very successful TV series. This sounded very interesting. I had never played a priest before.

So, without seeing the script, and the feeling that I owed John Goodrum a little something for letting me out of that last contract, I agreed. Not seeing the script first sometimes can throw up a few problems. This one did. When it finally arrived, I had a bit of a shock. The script itself consisted of sixty-nine pages, my character, "Father Brown", appears on sixty-four of them, never stopping to take a breath. Again, I did have three months to get it together, thank heavens, but still, for a man of my age, words do not go in as easily as they did when younger.

John did, I'm pleased to tell you, accommodate me by taking some of my lines and giving them to another character-relief all round. We rehearsed for two weeks up in Chesterfield (where Rumpus is based) before setting off on a three-month tour that took in lovely theatres and places like Malvern Festival Theatre, Windsor Theatre Royal, Theatre Royal Nottingham, And the beautiful Buxton Opera House. This was hard work and required a lot of concentration, but was progressing well until our last date, which was way up at the Forum Theatre Billingham. On the very last day of the tour, I awoke in the hotel with a terrible sore throat.

After trying my best to gargle with salt water, to little effect, I called down to John, who was staying in the same hotel, and he immediately suggested we go quickly to find the theatre doctor. Not that easy on a Saturday morning (probably out shopping with his wife at Tesco). Eventually, we did locate one, who examined my throat, said I was developing an acute case of laryngitis and gave me a throat spray in the hope of getting me through the two performances we had that day.

From the beginning of this tour, I did have an understudy, but this being the very last day, he had been let go the night before and was, by now, at home, in bed, with his feet up. Well, suffice to say, I did get through those two last shows, but the second one was an effort. As my performance went on, the voice was slowly becoming weaker and weaker, until, for the last twenty minutes, I'm not too sure I could be heard. That loss of voice lasted for the next three weeks at home, no voice - a strange feeling.

One of the great pleasures of working with Rumpus was meeting John's wife, Karen Henson. She, like John, runs her own touring company, "Tabs," in which again, like John, she writes, directs, and acts in various productions (can you imagine who wears the trousers in that household? Two directors?)

Once I had got my voice back and my strength, she offered me the part of the Inspector in "Dial M for Murder" at the Nottingham Playhouse. What a great play and production by Karen. Whilst playing in the evenings with that play, we rehearsed in the mornings a new play written by Karen, based loosely on the life of Marie Lloyd. This was set in a law court, depicting the trial of Marie, who had been accused of murder. This whole production took place in a real but unused courthouse, the Nottingham Assizes. What fun we had with that.

I myself played the old Judge (and of course, I went over the top) with a team of Tabs' regular actors. Susan Earnshaw, sparkling as Marie. Being performed in a real court meant that the audience was almost on top of us, which added greatly to the atmosphere. It was almost panto time. Unfortunately, the seating would only allow for two hundred and fifty at any time. We played for ten nights, but word of mouth was so good, we could have played another two weeks - what fun.

I have enjoyed working with both Rumpus and Tabs over the years. They look after me tremendously well (I suppose that goes with getting on a bit), and nothing is too much trouble. I will, if all goes well, be going out on tour with them once again soon, with a new version of "Father Brown" for a three-month tour around the country. I have, over those few years, covered quite a bit with both companies – drama, in a new play, again written by John Goodrum. ("The Eleventh Hour") Plus a very funny farce, "Caught in the Net" by Ray Cooney.

In that production, I witnessed one of the funniest performances I have ever seen in a play, George Telfer as Stanley. Great timing. Towards the end of the year, if theatres are still functioning after this pandemic, I shall set off with another new play, this time a political thriller, written by Hilary Bonner. We again shall be playing in theatres all over the country.

So, with Hilary's new play, "Father Brown" and the panto in Lowestoft, I think I have more than enough to keep me busy. Now dear reader, if at any time you see my name outside any theatre, in any town, please knock on the stage door, tell me you've read this book, and you can buy me a pint of Guinness.

164

John Lyons

I have been thinking for a couple of years now that the next panto I do will probably be my last. They do require a lot of energy and stamina. So, in the New Year, I will have a word with my knees and see if there is just one more left in me. I do hope so because I do enjoy all the fun we have. Plus, if I could get one close to London, and my great-nephews, Jake, Sonny Joe, Flynn and Izzy, could come and see their silly old uncle John, that would be a treat for me.

As a family, we are all very close. Laura, my daughter, lives very close with her husband Laurence. My elder brother Joe lives with his son Joseph very close, as do both his daughter Samantha, her husband Martin, with their kids, Flynn and Jake, and just a little further out, my nephew Christian, his wife Sophie, and Sonny Joe. It is lovely to have your family all living within touching distance. It means that we can do many things all together, like birthdays, picnics in the park, etc. Both Ann and I would miss all of that.

Unfortunately, both Ann`s sisters, Christine and Marilyn, live way out in the country. As I have said a few times, working in the theatre requires a lot of stamina. Throughout my life, I've always been a very physical person. Football, tennis, jogging etc. But, as with everyone, as the years began to catch up with me, those demanding sports went out the window, something less taxing needed to take their place. For many years my old friend, a man I have known for over forty years, actor/pop star Jess Conrad, had been nagging me to take up golf. Eventually, I did.

Jess, my boy, thank you. I have been playing now for about eight years, and I find that it has helped me greatly, especially my back. Most of the time I play down in Kent with a fine organiser, Mark Crane. The rest of the time, charity matches up and down the country.

Not Just George

Some lovely people play in these matches, not only actors and entertainers, the likes of Rick Wakeman, Bobby Davro but many sports stars, John Virgo, Peter Shilton, Sir Trevor Brooking, John H Stracey (world welterweight boxing champion) and Jess Conrad of course along with many more.

Over the years of giving my talks on P & O cruise ships, a lot of people would ask both myself and Ann, "Has John ever written a book?" I always gave the same answer. "No, I don`t think I could. I wouldn't have the patience or the dedication it takes to sit down every day and write." Remember, I'm a secondary schoolboy from the East End who hadn't even passed his eleven plus.

After a while, with the prompting of my wife, and Patsy Martin, my agent, I wrote a synopsis, which she, in turn, passed onwards, and a few people, to my surprise, took an interest. Then along came the pandemic, which put a hold on all work, and here I am. I started with a slight feeling of trepidation, but as I got further into it, I began to enjoy it. I can only hope that having read this little tale, you have enjoyed it too?

Once I got into the routine of writing, memories of people, places, and the work I have done over sixty years came flooding back. Many that I had not thought of for a long time. I have never kept a diary or book of my work, which is a shame because I'm sure over the period of all those years, there are some I have forgotten completely. Other jobs, and people, will come back to me in a few months' time, or my wife will remind me, but by then, too late, John. The last full stop will have been added.

I have, in my life been very lucky in many ways—my marriage, career, and family. I can't help but think that fate played a very big part. I look back and remember how I met my wife at the age of fifteen, how that changed the course of my life. A chance meeting with a journalist whilst playing football, who suggested I should try a drama school. Ready to walk away from my audition when stopped in my tracks by the drama teacher, from losing my nerve and going back to work with British Rail. How Ann and I stood outside a house when I said to her, "Wouldn't it be great to live there?" Fourteen years later, we moved into that very house. The night I ran left down Vallance Road, instead of right, and finished up collapsing on the doorstep of the Kray twins, who I'm sure saved my life.

It does make you wonder. Something that a stranger said to me once maybe sums it up. I was doing a tour of Holland with dear Bruce Alexander (who played Mullet in Frost) in big theatres in three different cities. When we reached the last night in Amsterdam, we both would take questions and answers after the audience had watched an episode of "Frost". Then we would relate certain anecdotes, finishing with, as many of the audience who wished, would line up, meet both of us on stage, have their photograph taken by a professional photographer, then leave.

It was surprising how many wished to take part, seeing as they all had to pay. Forty-five minutes or so had passed when a man in his thirties had his photo taken with me, said goodbye, said thank you for a wonderful show and left. Now, this, for me, stayed in my mind. He got about ten feet away, turned and said, "Mr Lyons, may I say something to you?"

"Yes, of course."

"You were born to be on the stage."Then left. Whether that is true or not, who knows, but it does make you think.

Not Just George

While working on my very first professional job, an old actress said to me, "John this is a very hard business you're in. If you can just make a living in this business, you're a success." WELL, I'VE MADE A LIVING.

I myself had never thought about writing this book. It was only people asking if I had done so on the cruise ships, plus the prompting of my wife and agent Patsy Martin, that got me thinking. Then along came COVID-19, which ruled out any jobs I had planned for the year. So, I buckled down.

For me, I thought the task would be like me decorating a room, that after a few hours, I would get tired of it and move on to something else. As I got more and more into it, and all those memories came flooding back, I began to enjoy it. I only hope, dear reader, that you have enjoyed coming along with me on my journey through life, as much as I have living it.

John Lyons

About the Author

John Lyons started his acting career as a founder member of the 'East 15 Acting School' in 1961. Upon leaving he went into the Professional company of the school 'Theatre Workshop' which at the time was under the direction of Joan Littlewood. In the intervening 50 years John's career has been both long and varied, covering both West End musicals and straight plays, including three separate years in 'The Mousetrap' and tours both in England and The Continent with the Musical " Oh! What a Lovely War"

His TV appearances are numerous (over 500) ranging from 'Upstairs Downstairs' Play for Today' 'The Sweeney' to 'On the Buses' 'George & Mildred' and 'The 19th Hole with Eric Sykes. John Lyons is of course best known for playing Sir David Jason's long suffering sidekick D.S. George Toolan in 'A Touch of Frost' which ran for a very successful 17 ½ years and currently being repeated daily on ITV3.

Panto has played a very big and fun time in John's life, starting in 1997 with productions of Dick Whittington and Aladdin with the Comedian Jim Davidson, playing Bristol. Palace Theatre Manchester, Mayflower Southampton etc, over a period of ten years.

During 2015 to present John has appeared in Cinderella, Aladdin, and Peter Pan, with John playing Capt Hook, for Paul Holman Associates. December 2014/January 2015 John appeared as 'King Crumble' in Sleeping Beauty at the Spa Theatre Bridlington. December 2016 saw John appearing as 'Baron Hardup' in 'Cinderella' at the Harlequin

Theatre, Redhill.

During 2018, John appeared as 'Father Brown' on tour throughout the UK in Rumpus Theatre's production of 'The Curse of The Invisible Man' and in 2021/22 will be appearing as 'Father Brown' in Rumpus Theatre production of 'The Murderer in the Mirror'. John has also toured in Rumpus Theatre productions in 'Caught in the Net' and 'The Eleventh Hour'.

In December 2018 and January 2019, John appeared again as 'King Crumble' in Paul Holman Associates production of 'Jack and the Beanstalk' at Bridlington Spa, and appeared during 2019 as 'Mr Brownlow' in Aberystwyth Arts Centre's production of 'Oliver'. December and January of 2019 John appeared as 'Baron Hardup' in Paul Holman Associates production of 'Cinderella'.

John is in great demand on the after dinner speaking circuit, personal appearances at 'On the Buses' reunions and numerous P & O Cruises talking about 'An actor's life - the beginning and conclusion' – 'The Touch of Frost Years' (his 17 years in a Touch of Frost with clips, outtakes, clips of pranks played on him).

A very busy and varied career I would say.